THROUGH
THEIR EYES

WORD WEAVERS

Edited By Elle Berry

First published in Great Britain in 2019 by:

Young Writers
Remus House
Coltsfoot Drive
Peterborough
PE2 9BF
Telephone: 01733 890066
Website: www.youngwriters.co.uk

Printed and bound in the UK by BookPrintingUK
Website: www.bookprintinguk.com
YB04260

FOREWORD

Since 1991, here at Young Writers we have celebrated the awesome power of creative writing, especially in young adults, where it can serve as a vital method of expressing strong (and sometimes difficult) emotions, a conduit to develop empathy, and a safe, non-judgemental place to explore one's own place in the world. With every poem we see the effort and thought that each pupil published in this book has put into their work and by creating this anthology we hope to encourage them further with the ultimate goal of sparking a life-long love of writing.

Through Their Eyes challenged young writers to open their minds and pen bold, powerful poems from the points-of-view of any person or concept they could imagine – from celebrities and politicians to animals and inanimate objects, or even just to give us a glimpse of the world as they experience it. The result is this fierce collection of poetry that by turns questions injustice, imagines the innermost thoughts of influential figures or simply has fun.

The nature of the topic means that contentious or controversial figures may have been chosen as the narrators, and as such some poems may contain views or thoughts that, although may represent those of the person being written about, by no means reflect the opinions or feelings of either the author or us here at Young Writers.

We encourage young writers to express themselves and address subjects that matter to them, which sometimes means writing about sensitive or difficult topics. If you have been affected by any issues raised in this book, details on where to find help can be found at *www.youngwriters.co.uk/info/other/contact-lines*

CONTENTS

Aoife Jordan (11) 68
Bo Macdonald (12) 69
Anna Isabella Hope (11) 70
Neve Weir (11) 71
Emily Laird (11) 72

Dalkeith High School, Dalkeith

Isla Smith (11) 73
Amy Robb (11) 74
Thomas Roy (12) 76

Dereham Neatherd High School, Dereham

Alyssa Baines (13) 77
Dali Sophia Brady (12) 78
Sam Goward (11) 79

Dover College, Dover

Nathaniel James Turner (13) 81
Belle Klappa (14) 82
August Moos (13) 83
Avy Taylor (13) 84
Samuel James Smith (13) 85
Scarlett Rathmell (13) 86
Rishma Patel (13) 87

Greenfields School, Forest Row

Isabel Bird (13) 88
Reese Elan Wilson (12) 89
Porscha Smith (12) 90
Sophia Garcia (13) 91
Lulu Gabriella Borg (14) 92

Heston Community School, Heston

Parjot Sandhu (13) 93
Omolara Zainab Moloney (13) 94
Dhruv Kirtesh Shah (13) 96
Nancy Sunil Dutt (13) 97
Karanveer Sondh (13) 98
Taysier Sami (12) 99

Gursimran Kaur Chouhan (12) 100
Adeline Sam (13) 101
Imaan Akhtar (13) 102
Yunis Haider (13) 103
Herneet Kaur Gaba (12) 104
Jasmeen Kaur (12) 105
Arjan Athwal (13) 106
Gabriela Ujma (13) 107
Octavio Pinto (13) 108
Dylan Afonso (13) 109
Navdeep Kaur Kharay (12) 110
Pakeeza Siddiqui (13) 111
Pavleen Madhan (12) 112
Aamna Ali (13) 113

Kingsmead School, Hoylake

Eddie Thomas (15) 114
Jack Oliver Hall (11) 119

Loxford School, Ilford

Anusha Tahir (15) 120
Amanjit Singh (15) 122
Alisha Gulrez 124
Simran Patti 125
Erica Hossain 126
Sophie Davouloury (15) 128
Iman Nasir (15) 129
Amandeep Manku (16) 130
Aisha Ahmed (15) 131
Zainab Hamid 132
Eesha Nadeem (15) 133
Amaya Ruckmal 134
Tafanique Service 135

Madani Girls' School, Whitechapel

Safiyyah Islam (12) 136
Abida Ahmed (12) 138
Jannat Basith (12) 139
Samiyyah Najiba (13) 140

Gabriel Whelpton (14)	203
Jonny Wainhouse (13)	204
Henry Watson (14)	205
George Henry Clark (13)	206
Callum Griffith (13)	207
George Maniadakis (14)	208
Jake Ford (14)	209

The Stanway School, Stanway

Hannah Cain	210
Oriana Barnard (12)	211
Martha Elliot (13)	212
Samuel Thompson (12)	214

The Tiffin Girls' School, Kingston Upon Thames

| Sivanky Uthayakumar (14) | 215 |

Wellington School, Ayr

Jonathan Dunn	216
Erin Ward	218
Zoë Rosalyn Glen (11)	219
Megan Seales (11)	220
Emma Henderson (11)	222
Annabel Elizabeth Barrett (12)	223
Khalan Thomas Lendrum (12)	224
Sophia Girgis	225
Tansy Allan (12)	226
Charlotte Hardy (12)	227
Anna Hunter (12)	228
Benjamin Richmond	229
Fraser Steward	230

THE
POEMS

How I Wish

Oh, how I wish to have my sapphire and basil touch,
My wind and breezy days.
My fern forests packed with trees and life,
My calm and safe atmosphere for whom I thought I trusted.
How I wish to have my beauty back,
My creations and my animals,
Everything decorated just for me.
That, however, is only hope,
Hope that might not perform itself.
And that, I've been longing for a long time now.
My glaciers are shattering,
My water is flooding,
My trees are falling,
I am dying.
I scream, beg for mercy,
My voice is not heard but is heard by the people who speak
for my pain and anguish.
They are ones who care,
They are ones who value their future.
And yet, I am the home and soil of those who have betrayed
me.
Those who have turned me into who I am now.
I still have aspirations, and that will continue for eighteen
more months.
My people are truly dear to me, but am I dearest to them?
Oh, how I wish to be Earth again.

Noor Alrefai (12)
Bentley Wood High School, Stanmore

Trapped

Trapped, my own skin -
the thick, grey
metal bars restraining me.
My bones, my skin, a prison.
But I am not a criminal.

A life sentence
In a cold prison cell
Could never compare to this constant torment.
Hell! My soul was being torn apart.
Killing me slowly.

I'm trapped.
In Hell.
Worse.

I am the sun - bright, radiant -
behind the dark grey clouds.
Trapped.
You can't see me.
My light won't shine that far.
The mask that covers my scars, the anger, the pain, the
needing to belong
That's what you see -
That is not me.

I'm a prisoner -
In my own bones, flesh and skin.

I live in Hell.
Get me out! I constantly shout but no one can hear me.
I swallow the pain and aim for a bright future,

A future as bright as the sun
In my dreams, I am as free as a bird,
Soaring through the sky.
Freedom.
Freedom is all I wish for.

Wishes.
They never come but...
I wish I lived in a world where I could be myself.
A world where I don't have to hide my scars
And pretend that everything is okay.
But social pressure is consuming me,
The need to fit in, the need to be someone I'm not.

Trapped.
I try to break free from these heavy, metal chains.
But I am not brave, nor courageous.
I will die unknown.
No one will see my light, my true colours
The mask is not me!

Trapped.
I want to make a change.
No one should feel this way.
At least not every day

No one should suffer for being different.
No one should feel as if they don't belong.
I am not an outcast.
I am the sun - bright and radiant.
Behind the dark grey clouds.

Eileen Naa Korkoi Magnusen (13)
Bentley Wood High School, Stanmore

History's Spoken Word

Apartheid,
The laws separating blacks from whites
Poorer from richer
Me against the harsh world, a fight against segregation
I was born in July of 1918, me, Nelson Mandela
No one would ever think of what I could accomplish
What I would become
Enclosed in the rigorous, unforgiving hands of the truth
We knew there would be a fight for freedom

We stood side by side, hand in hand
Not knowing of the future
1962, I was arrested for trying to overthrow the state
Just like that, *boom!* hope gone
Twenty-seven years of hard labour, all for what?
Wanting freedom?
1990 brought a new spring of unity,
This was the year I was released from the restricting chains
of prison

We protested through bitter winters, humid summers and
beautiful springs
Not once did we give up
The revolutionary changes
Later in 1994, I became president
Apartheid was made to separate us
Instead, it brought us closer together.

Jasmine Marshall-Bouaouina (11)
Bentley Wood High School, Stanmore

Dark Eyes

I walk
I walk and walk, but never talk
People turn their heads
But they don't realise I'm dead
I'm black
That's why
My skin tells my story
But also puts up a wall
It shows my history
But leaves me with mystery
Did you know that I am smart?
No, because you couldn't find a part
For me in the job that I'm good at
Because I'm black!
You can deny it
But you put me in that ditch
The day you saw me for me.
I'd like to think the world could change
But that would have to be arranged
Because people are still afraid
Of what my skin colour represents
When you stare into my eyes,
All you can see is darkness
Even when my eyes are shining bright
I look back at you and wonder
Do you wish I was blonder?

Would it be so hard
To send me a welcoming card?
When I look back on life
I could have been stabbed by a knife
Because all there is is hate
No one is anyone's mate
If we all got together
Maybe it would change the weather
From the horrible rain
To a place without pain
My dreams will never come true
When all everybody can see is you
Yes, your beautiful blue eyes shimmer in darkness
But all people can see is my blackness.
If you looked deeper, my eyes are beautiful too,
They're just not blue!
The day's over and my eyes are closing
And I'm finally at peace.

Naomi Ogunniyi (13)
Bentley Wood High School, Stanmore

Those That Are There For Me

There are millions of stars which lie in the sky
Overlooking the world in the darkness of night
There are millions of planets that spin and fly
Which circle the sun at an amazing height.

There are 195 countries with different styles
All scattered around the world, some big, some small
There are different homes with different smiles
With different people, short and tall.

There are billions of people within these places
Who keep their loved ones in their hearts
With different cultures and different ages
Even though they might be miles apart.

There are seven continents I can guarantee
With languages like English, Spanish or Greek
But I know that there's only one of me
And I know that I'm unique.

Yet I still look up to people
Those that I can't live without
And even though we're all equal
They are people that to me stand out.

My sister, my mum and dad
My friends, my family too
They cheer me up when I'm sad
And I know that it is true.

They are my heroes in this world I live in
The people that support my dreams
Whenever I'm down, they make me grin
The people that make me beam.

Abigail Caniparu (12)
Bentley Wood High School, Stanmore

The Forest Disease

The wind drifts lazily across my home
Or rather the barren landscape beyond me with charred
skeletons
The radiant colours are replaced with monochrome
My branches rustle quietly
The humans left me all alone
Said I was too big to handle gingerly
But my day is coming
A scent of sulphur and carbon slithers in the air
Like a snake in wait, sneering
The scent's good friend silence is here
Unlike him, he jerks uncontrollably in the air
Wanting all to know he's there
His raucous chatter echoes
As he floats away to another place
Skittering across the leaves are a group of wide-eyed
geckos
Silence is here no more
But the geckos scatter as the rev of machine
Approach me armed with a saw
My branches rustle as the wind roars past the disarray
All the noise sounds like a heartbeat
Beating steadily away
But everything is becoming quieter now
Like cotton is numbing my senses
I can see the Earth below me

A beautiful Earth
And
Now
All
Is
Dark.

Maryam Abdalla (13)

Bentley Wood High School, Stanmore

How You See Me

Look at me
What do you wonder?
You see the scarf around my head
And my hijab
You may call me a terrorist
You may call me a killer
You may hate me but most of all
You know my heart is full of love
I'm not like the others
I'm not who you believe
You judge me like the cover of a book
You don't see the real me because you don't listen
If you were to open your eyes and ears
You'd hear a different story
You'd hear the sad songs of my tears and the story of my
pain
I'm just like the girl in your neighbourhood
I'm just like your daughter
I want to learn and live a happy life
I want to change how the world sees me
But you only shut me out
For not even my own actions
Look at me but don't judge me from how I look
Like a cover but give me a chance to speak
And listen to my unheard voice
Listen to the woe of my heart

Look at me, now
What do you wonder?

Shabnam Tasmim (13)
Bentley Wood High School, Stanmore

Blind

What a wonderful president America has!
The best since 20th January 2017
The only president to care about the hole in the wall
Never did care about the hole in the ozone.

Ozone? Never heard of that?
Looks like he has done a really good job protecting you
Climate change?
Oh, don't worry about that either
That doesn't exist.

A modern-day tyrant
That seems about right

His tyrannical views have spread like the California wildfires
Along with the toxic fumes
The toxic fumes that are painfully congesting the Earth

All these major issues have been clearly overlooked
Overlooked by one who's never stuck their nose in a book
Isn't it wonderful?
Trump, do you agree?

Don't worry fellow Brexiteers
We're not that far behind
We're all following the leader wherever he might go
His doppelgänger has made himself comfy.

Tinhinan Souak (15)
Bentley Wood High School, Stanmore

Lennie's Done A Bad Thing

This evil grimace seemed to trail along the tracks of my face
With cruel words imprisoned behind my gritted bars of teeth
A toxic friend twisted into a wholesome enemy
He's really done it this time

He's not like these other guys
I struggled to plant the patches in his mind with seeds of the
American dream
I tried to distract him, by snatching his fantasy
He would reach his reality in a higher place up in the sky
I'm just like these other guys
Happily, I'll replace a trickle of blood with an endless stream
of shallow water

My mind and hand were neck and neck
In this race of anticipation
That is until my mind took a needless slip, pushing my hand
straight forward into first place
And straight down onto the trigger

Without a quiver, I watched the crimson drop from out his
neck
While the bunch of vacant souls gush in.

Morgan Davis (14)
Bentley Wood High School, Stanmore

The Words You Say

The words you say make me really sad
When the truth is, I haven't done anything bad
Sometimes the words that hurt me the most
Often start off as a joke or a boast.

The words you say make my spine shiver
When I talk in front of you, my lips quiver
You bully me just to look cool
Don't you know you just look like a fool?

The words you say make me skip most days of school
I even tried to drown myself in the pool
I think about the things you say every night
I quickly hide or run at your sight.

The words you say make me cry
Crying makes my throat very dry
Why can nobody hear my scream?
It gets so bad that you appear in my dream.

The words you say have made me had enough
I will release myself from this handcuff
I have found the courage to tell
Now hopefully things will turn out well.

Rakia Sufizada (13)
Bentley Wood High School, Stanmore

Held Captive

Being in jail is lonely at night
It's waiting for letters that no one will write
It's depending on people you thought were your friends
When they fail to come through again and again.

It's sitting around with nothing to do
Trying to figure out just who is who
It's finding out that hearts are made of stone
And realising that you're all alone.

It's waiting for visits that never take place
From so-called friends who've forgotten your face
It's wondering why time's moving so slow
And every dream you have has no place to go.

Therefore I will do my time with my head held high
And keep my integrity and pride until the day I die
The day will come when I am free
Then it will be my turn to forget those who forget me.

Sara Maliqi (11)
Bentley Wood High School, Stanmore

The Cost Of Beauty

She runs
She cries
She begs
She tries

But nothing
No nothing
Seems to work

Through the forest and out the gates
But still trapped in her world of hate
Down the valley and out of the doors
But she knows she can't escape the wars

Follow the light of a camera's flash
But 'twas only a dream and woke up in his bed

Her rouged lips and apple-red cheeks
Concealed every present received within a week
Only a hush and a shush will send her back in her place
Of working for a man who comes back home late

Sealing her mouth with a swipe of lipstick
Doesn't fear hell but only what she speaks of it
As she knows her demon is sleeping beside her

She ran
She cried
She begged

But she died

Beauty is left in the ugly.

Megan Groza (13)
Bentley Wood High School, Stanmore

Rosa Parks

My story starts in 1955
When black people every day had to sit patiently at the
back of the bus
Then one day a bus driver came to me and asked,
Could you move so this kind man could have a seat?
And I replied with only one word... "No."
He asked me again more forcefully
I still refused, holding onto my dignity

Almost three minutes later, he had called the police
It was in December that I was arrested
But I made a change and something started
The Bus Boycott
All of a sudden, I felt scared but I felt reassured
For equality...

It was a time when people stopped using the bus
The money earned by the bus drivers got lower
I was proud to see the difference
It might have been something small
But it made a big difference.

Sophie Murugi Muriithi (11)
Bentley Wood High School, Stanmore

A Harsh Teen Life

Being a teen
Well, everyone thinks we're mean
To be honest, we are never seen
We've tried to be heard
But they just run away like birds.

The only time when I couldn't eat my food
Was when I was in a mood
I've been followed and unfollowed
By new and old.

I've been bullied
I've been a voice
All I had to do was make the right choice
There have also been times
Where I've been stuck in slime.

I've been mistaken
And overtaken
I've been quiet
Whilst I've been on a diet
I've been sly and made people cry.

I've been a mess
Whilst being stressed
I've been in a bubble
And been in trouble.

It's a rushed and harsh teen life.

Abidha Islam (11)
Bentley Wood High School, Stanmore

Through The Cage

I sat down on my armchair
To answer the phone call
From my brother from prison
From stealing to killing
From fear to terror
From the mistakes from the past
And all hope was lost

Tears in my eyes as I sat down
In horror and pain
In agony, crying from sleepless nights
Wishing for my brother to be free
But never noticed how he will never change
As he killed and kidnapped people
Joined gangs and sold drugs
In his eyes, I was useless,
He just used me to protect him

I sat down on my armchair,
Learning the truth from my brother
That he never loved me
Until he was in prison for his actions
And what I learnt from him is that
From your actions, there are consequences.

Ayan Hussein (11)
Bentley Wood High School, Stanmore

Our Love

I am your mother
The one who raised you
You are the twinkle that shines above
This is what brings our love.

We are paper stuck together
Remember, I love you forever
You are a precious jewel
Much shinier than a metal tool.

A piece of my heart belongs to you
Our hearts have been stuck with glue
I remember when you used to giggle
In fact, you still do this today
It's official.

Together, we can be a team
My wish for you is to achieve your dreams.

I am your mother
The one who raised you
You are the twinkle that shines above
This is what brings our love.

Fatima Faisal Iftikhar (12)
Bentley Wood High School, Stanmore

Eyes Of Truth

(Through the eyes of a phone screen)

We see the truth
We witness the lies
We are the eyes.

If we had mouths
We'd never stop talking
Because we see the truth
We witness the lies
We are the eyes.

Through your masks
There are black souls that we see.

Every lie
Every truth
They don't know which is which
But us, the eyes, we always know.

When we see a person's eyes
It exposes the truth.

Is this why they say
Look me in the eyes
Only speak the truth
Lies can hurt forever
Some hearts get too torn to mend.

We see the truth
We witness the lies
We are the eyes.

Israa Abood (12)
Bentley Wood High School, Stanmore

Trained Feral

I know that I am one of the lucky ones
I should be thankful
I could have had my leg sawed off with scissors
I could have had my eyes stolen from me
I could no longer exist
I know that I am lucky
Are the bars in front of me for my protection of others?
I used to run free in my forest with my brothers
But I will run free in my forest with my brothers
But I will never see them ever again
I know that I am the lucky one
I know that I am sheltered yet I feel homeless
I know that I am fed yet I feel empty
Where did I go wrong? How did I hurt my family? Why am I
imprisoned?
Am I really the lucky one?

Charlotte O'Reilly
Bentley Wood High School, Stanmore

Fame: Won And Gone

(Through the eyes of a wedding dress)

Today's the day
I can see a flower bouquet
My chance of fame
Won't be the same.

For today is the wedding day
I sparkle and shine
As I walk down the aisle.

People stare at me in awe
Although I'm only shown with shoes and jewellery
I'm happy there's no cruelty... for now.

My fame won and...
Now it's gone
Stored at the back of the cupboard
Now I will never see the light of day
They all celebrate without me
I wonder when I'll be free.

I shout, "Help!"
But nobody comes
My fame won
And now it's gone.

Ruqayyah Nifal (12)
Bentley Wood High School, Stanmore

An Unlucky Fly

An unlucky fly
Innocent as could be
Not a beautiful butterfly
Or a luxurious bee.

It has no bold colour
And has no form of pattern
It's frequently in the summer
But it's quite forgotten.

But when it comes to dodging
We're masters of that
Other creatures end up failing
And we bring it as a fact.

But when they squirt the *spray*...
As called 'antibacterial'
It clearly ends my day
And I have to do a funeral.

We're targeted for no reason
As you can see
A little itsy, bitsy fly
That's the story of me!

Luna Aisha Spadaro (11)
Bentley Wood High School, Stanmore

Truth

She cries and cries
But there is no use
Until someone
Reveals the truth.

No one listens to her
Nor is she seen
People act
As if she is a bean.

This is a story
About a true woman
Who had to suffer
To get what she is given.

Everything's sweet
And everything's nice
But some people
Can't open their eyes.

Soft and cuddly
Warm and wanting
She can be someone
Who is always stunning.

Just open your eyes
A little more
So that you can see
What's behind the door.

Ghezal Saee (13)
Bentley Wood High School, Stanmore

The Life Of A Phone

I text for people night and day
I scroll through arguments just like a play
Tears, joy, bullies and grades
They're all expressions that are part of a phase

I hide behind a screen protector
All cold and lonely
I wear a sparkly pink case
Looking like a pony

I watch over people who bully and hate
Not able to stop them
Yet sympathise and rate
Comments, likes, dislikes and judging
It's all my fault without people knowing!

My life is terrible
No one can relate
I'm just a stupid platform
That causes lots of hate.

Sarah Yunesi
Bentley Wood High School, Stanmore

Lights, Camera, Action

Blinking in amazement, dazzled by the lights
What *is* this place, did my satnav get it right?
Masters bellowing orders to the servants
Ants scurrying rapidly, fixing the curtains.

Face-painted ladies, peering in the mirror
An army approaching nearer and nearer
Sounds like a thunderstorm, people screaming to each other
I feel pain in my ears, should I even *bother*?

My heart is pounding in my head
I don't want a sanction
But then I hear the thrilling words,
"Emma Watson, lights, camera, action."

Huda Huquqi (12)
Bentley Wood High School, Stanmore

Politician's Point Of View

I'll tell you a secret
A deep, deep secret
As deep as despair
As sweet as a treat
But let's keep it discreet.

My boss won't listen,
Not even a peep
Yet I have tried and tried yet again
I have even tried shouting
Now I have started doubting.

I'll tell you a secret
A deep, deep secret
As deep as despair
As sweet as a treat
But let's keep it discreet.

This is my truth
My sad, upsetting truth
For no one will listen
Not even a youth
This is my sad, sad truth.

Hiba Kola (12)
Bentley Wood High School, Stanmore

Be Innocent But Be A Lion Inside

I'm writing these poems
From inside a lion
And it's really dark in here
So please excuse the handwriting
Which might not be clear.

In the jungle as I roar
Loud rumbling from my core
Magnificent mane of golden brown
I am the king but I wear no crown.

Predators and enemies, they have two
Human hunters, hyenas too
Lions like me and our lioness pride
If you cross us, run, don't hide!

Samreen Jabarkhyl (11)
Bentley Wood High School, Stanmore

If I Was A Superhero

If I was a superhero
I would definitely fly
All the way up to the sky
Way up high.

If I was a superhero
I'd have special powers
Flying over towers
Never going lower.

If I was a superhero
I'd help all of the poor
Give them food, more
And make them hungry no more.

If I was a superhero
I'm sure you'll agree
I am me
I'm happy to be free.

Suhaila Adam (11)
Bentley Wood High School, Stanmore

Vampire

I am different from others
I give them shivers
I am as pale as snow
I don't want them to know.

Am I different? Am I lost?
I don't know as I'm as cold as frost
I wish I had a heart beating
While I was sleeping
But I know that's not for a vampire.

I have a secret
I'm not allowed to share it
I'm a vampire
And nobody knows it.

Almeera Hussain (11)
Bentley Wood High School, Stanmore

A Message To My Friend

This is a message to my friend, Pizza
It's true, I would never leave ya
Even if I turned brown
And the sun went down
We would stay together
Like salt and pepper.

Ismah Jamil (12)
Bentley Wood High School, Stanmore

Optical Illusions

Optical illusions make you think,
They sometimes also make you blink,
Sometimes they have two meanings,
Sometimes they can be deceiving.

Optical illusions are interesting to look at,
They can be confusing, but don't mind that,
Sometimes arguments start to spread,
For people think differently in their head.

People think optical illusions are cool,
They are designed to try and fool,
I can't seem to think what they're all about,
Maybe someday, I'll figure it out.

Optical illusions are good for the brain,
No two illusions are the same,
Optical illusions are really fun,
They're all so different, every one.

Heather Little (12)
Berwickshire High School, Langtongate

To The Day I Die

To the day you die, you shall never cry,
My mother used to sing to me at night,
"Get up on your feet, never accept defeat!"
But ages come and go and my childhood is long ago,
I tried to bring my ideals to life during teenage strife,
But that didn't stop the knife,
That nearly took my life while defending my pride,
Thus ended the prime of my life.

Then I found the one I loved,
Kissed and made up with all my quarrels,
And when things got too hard to push back,
I was always there to hold, even if I was 'so old'!
Now I have to say goodbye,
They're all grown up, out at night,
While I wonder if they're alright.

Now my back hurts all the time, my hair's going white,
And I'm wondering if the end is in sight,
My time is ticking down,
Like my mum's *tsk* when she frowned.

When I look around,
Everything else is anything but safe and sound,
Danger looms all around,
The rainforest burns and the doomsday clock ticks down,
Like Death's mocking laughter mocking me while I'm down.

Well shame to you, those that would burn us down, accept
defeat,
Let your shoulders sag with the weight and heat,
Because my mum always said, just as I went to bed,
"No matter how dark the night,
You will always bring the light,
My little shining knight."

So I pass the torch to you, generation after me,
Please do better than me and always remember to get on
your feet,
Never accept defeat,
Stand tall, never give in to them all,
Because the demons of strife will scream,
But never let their mockery get past your beautiful sheen,
To not be tired with this world is a gift you must use well,
So go on, my angels, and tell them the truth,
That the light will always shine through.

Robert Morton (13)
Berwickshire High School, Langtongate

Wee Jock

Another day dawns with worry and pain,
I go to the cupboard for food, but remember there's nane.
I stand in the queue wi ma wee ration book,
Nae sweets I bet, I'm feared tae look!
I come from the city, but had tae leave ma hame,
My possessions in a bag, I boarded the train.
I live wi a new family, oh, they are quite nice,
But it's on a farm and there are loads of mice!
It's all Hitler's blame that I had to leave my mum and dad,
He's dropping bombs all over, I think he's bad.

Four years later and I'm still here,
This war has caused heartache and many a tear.
I'm now a young man and carry a gun,
But I've lost ma childhood... it should have been fun...
One day soon, I may go back to my city,
But things have changed, mair's the pity.
Ma mum and dad were still in the toon,
When the air raid siren sounded, they had to run
underground.
Mum made it in time, but Dad was late,
That sad day, he met his fate.
He heard it coming, the German plane overhead,
But they dropped the bomb and now he's dead.
Mum went soon after in a similar way,
So on this farm, I will have to stay an orphan.
I'm only fourteen and very sad,

This war has cost me my mum and dad.
At night when I'm alone, lying in ma bed,
It's the thought of soldiers and guns that fills ma head.
This war has changed me... I don't want to fight,
I wish it was over and things would be alright.
But another day dawns, I dream of the day,
When it's all peace and happiness and I can go oot to play.
I'm still waiting...
Wee Jock.

Aaron Richardson (15)
Berwickshire High School, Langtongate

A Note

A note.

What do you do when you don't
want to die
but you don't always
want to live

When life is beautiful enough
to keep you
focused.

Hope is strong enough
to pull you up and love is
wet enough
to stay on your tongue
But nothing is strong enough
to drown out

your thoughts.

So I often find myself
pouring over pictures
of happy faces
overhearing happy conversations
and watching
casual giggles in the evening and think
is it real?

Well they all decide to
tell me just to stop
thinking
about it
well
until they feel some big monster laughing
at their every move
then they can tell me
it's all in my head.

Miya Carlin (13)
Berwickshire High School, Langtongate

Forgiveness

I look into her eyes,
darkness swirls around like a tornado,
hidden dark tunnels appear,
secrets and pain engraved into the soul,
the thorns of pain and sorrow wrap around,
like spikes puncturing hope,
the chamber of freedom interlocked with sin,
if only that angelic beam of sun would shine upon our eyes,
the key to joy and peace,
that would shatter all the hideous deeds to bits.
If only people knew how to forgive!

Frances Walmsley (13)
Berwickshire High School, Langtongate

Still And Sturdy

Standing still and sturdy,
Holding together bricks,
I've been here for ages,
Watching the children play,

Playing tennis with me,
Passing a ball to me,
Climbing up my bricks
And leaning against me,

I've watched the children grow,
I've watched the children play,
But not noticing me,
I'm just a lonely wall,

But, now, I am too old,
My bricks will start to crack,
As I tumble to my death
All I see is the old bricks,

But the children don't care
And they still keep playing
And after all, I am...
Just an old brick wall.

Amelia Hopkins (11)
Bromley High School, Bickley

Just A Stick With A Graphite Core

I am just a tiny, little stick with a graphite core,
Many people will use me for writing and drawing,
They will bite and chew on me, until my blunt end becomes gnarly and short,
Then, I will be tossed to one side, never to be seen again.

I am just a tiny little stick with a graphite core,
Many children will use me to make a map of their imagination,
They won't cherish me, but I will help them until the end of my short lifespan,
Then, they will start using a pen and leave me in solitude.

I am just a humble pencil,
Many artists will love me and will keep me in a metal case so I don't snap,
They will treasure me and create amazing masterpieces with me,
Then, when I become too short and stubby, I will be tossed in the bin like all the others.

I am a spectacular invention,
Many people underestimate me,
They underestimate the power of creativity and of a single word on paper,
The power that I hold is second to none.

I am a tiny, unimportant stick with a graphite core,
Nobody uses me anymore,

All the infants and children just want electronics, not writing
sets,
Even the artists rarely use me,
Few remember how I showed them unconditional love,
They just know that a computer is faster,
More efficient than me,
I am just a cylindrical piece of wood with a graphite core-
As the computers define me,
Hurled into the corner of your bedside drawer.

Shreya Aravinthan (13)
Bromley High School, Bickley

Alone

Through my eyes I see
A group without me,
I feel isolated
Alone,
Bullied.

They look up and I smile,
They snicker,
I feel isolated,
Alone,
Bullied.

No one cares about me,
How I feel or what I see,
I feel isolated,
Alone,
Bullied.

The world moves on fast,
Yet I stay the same
I feel isolated,
Alone,
Bullied.

Lucksha Ananda (11)
Bromley High School, Bickley

Behind Doors

All I can do is cry myself to sleep at night
Wishing for it all to stop - worthless is how I feel
My friends are the only thing making me feel alright
Things that you have made me do, like stealing their meals

I have one question, why me? Why?
Are you proud of yourself?
Are you proud of what you've done?
You put me down and make me not want to fly high
There's nothing else left for me, there's no fun

Your life may be hard but I don't deserve that
Look what you have done to me, to everyone
You've made my life a living Hell
But I listen to you and don't tell

I wish there was a door I could hide behind
I don't want to be stuck here forever
Maybe there's a place out there where I can stay
And no one will find me - never mind

You do it to me every day, are you ever going to stop?
Or not?
Now look, your friends are here too
The things you have done to me, I have not forgotten
It's not just you, it's all of your crew.

Katie Louise Flowers (12)
Cleethorpes Academy, Cleethorpes

Young Hero

Superheroes are supposed to be strong.
They're supposed to save people

But I'm not strong, I'm weak.
Why else would I let everyone hurt me?
Push me, call me names?

If I were strong, I wouldn't be haunted by my power.
The future mocks me, giving me vague views
That leave my skin crawling...

Like the time it showed a tree burning,
Making me think something bad
Would happen to my teammates.

I spent weeks in cold fear,
Only to realise my vision was
Foreshadowing a petty argument.

If I were strong, I would be repulsed
At the thought of eating,
I wouldn't look at myself in the mirror in disgust.

I don't even know who I am anymore.

Am I the superhero the city loves, or am I a scared teen
That hasn't learnt much about life?

I'll ask you this: *how am I supposed to save people*
If I can't save myself?

Nairobi Marin Burke (13)
Cleethorpes Academy, Cleethorpes

Hero

Once in the dark stood a wise, old oak,
Its branches reaching up towards the sky.
Answers, it was looking for,
Answers to the dark side of life.

But not at once did he find them,
Only after days, months and years of searching,
Hard work and dedication were required,
And that he gave.

For the saplings needed him to survive,
Many needed his answers,
Until one day he reached the light,
A hero and a lifesaver.

The oak tree, a selfless and heroic soul,
Who transformed the lives of many.
For the oak tree was a scientist,
And the saplings were the people,
The people who he cured,
And the people whose lives he changed forever.

Isabella Griffiths (12)
Cleethorpes Academy, Cleethorpes

Autumn

Autumn is coming. It is almost here.
It is now October and summer is over.
The wind is blowing and the night is growing.
The leaves are coming down,
Making a carpet: red-orange and brown.
I dance with the leaves down the street,
And I shuffle through them with my feet.
I walk through the cool breeze,
And then I let out a small sneeze.
I hurry back home so I can sit by the heat,
I can sip hot chocolate whilst I eat.
I stare out of the window and see some leaves,
The pile is so big, it's hard to believe.
I run towards it and fly through the air,
I dive so deep, there are leaves in my hair.
Autumn has come. It is finally here.

Wilma Meyerhoff (11)
Cleethorpes Academy, Cleethorpes

Bullying Hurts

You are unique and confident,
I wonder why people enjoy bullying
I hear the sound of teasing and laughing
I hear the sound of running and hiding

They pretend words don't hurt
They keep their tears inside
They shake and hide because they're nervous
They cry when they're alone

Don't be afraid
Stand up for yourself
You are worth it, don't cry
It's not you, it's them

If you have a mind
You wouldn't stand and watch people cry
They laugh through their tears
They pretend they're fine
You know they're hurting.

Amie Moran (11)
Cleethorpes Academy, Cleethorpes

Mental Health Nurse

You're a mum, a dad, someone
If you feel you can't cope
Don't put a full stop on it
Dream and hope

It's okay to be sad
Or even in despair
Don't worry too much
Because people are always there

Stress
Bipolar disorder
Drugs
Body dysmorphic disorder

Be strong in each and every hour
It is the first time and will be the last
Be proud of your power
Imagine you're a hero in a cape

Don't leave a short story
With words of your pain
But a story of strength
And the things you can gain.

Luna Anais Camille Coret (11)
Cleethorpes Academy, Cleethorpes

A Soldier's Life

In a soldier's life,
You kiss goodbye to your wife.
Not knowing when,
You'll ever see her again.

In a soldier's life,
You friend is your knife,
Right by your side,
As you march on with pride.

A soldier's life,
Is full of trouble and strife,
Leaving children behind,
To fight the fight for mankind.

In a soldier's life,
There are no comfortable pillows
But they go to bed,
Being our heroes.

A soldier's life,
Is full of sacrifice,
But what is the price,
Of a human life?

Millie-Mae Roberts (11)
Cleethorpes Academy, Cleethorpes

Friends

I couldn't understand,
Not at the time.
The hands on the clock
Stopped climbing around,
All I could hear,
Was an echoing sound.
The voices of my so-called friends,
The ones who were always by my side,
'Never' once made me cry
What was that in their hands?
Why were they telling me to eat what I'm given?
Was this a toxin in them
That was hidden?
What had this party become?
Was it real or was I dumb?
I wanna go home
Though I might go free
There's nobody here to help me.

Lilla Jazmin Portas (11)
Cleethorpes Academy, Cleethorpes

Future With Friends

F lying saucers zooming past me but me alone

J **U** piter, where I would like to be with my friends and family

T ime machines showing me when I had a BFF

Astrona **U** t, what I wanted to be, but no one believed in me

R ight over there, I see something, people who want to play

E very day I want to play, today is that day.

Luke Bucknole (11)
Cleethorpes Academy, Cleethorpes

My Hero!

My dad and I have special bonds,
It's clear you didn't know,
And when we are together,
Our super bond grows.

We have the power of emotions,
To push through our sadness,
Our other talent is:
To remain calm through the madness.

I'm growing even more,
With each passing hour,
As you didn't know,
We still have our powers!

When I'm fully grown,
I know I'll be glad,
That I owned my own special and talented hero,
My best friend, my dad.

Tiegan Gordon (11)
Cleethorpes Academy, Cleethorpes

Stop And Think

Sometimes you need to stop and think,
I saw some people spray-painting on a wall under a bridge,
One of them wasn't sure whether to join in,
He started to join them by spray painting but they were
caught,
They narrowly escaped but I knew one of them,
The one who wasn't sure,
He grew a guilty conscience and he grew so guilty,
That he confessed and got into lots of trouble,
That's why you have to stop and think,
Think about what you do.

Ashton Smith (11)

Cleethorpes Academy, Cleethorpes

That Girl

See that girl? Yes, the one with the 'smile'.
Little do you know, she's been hurt for a while
'Too fat', 'too ugly', why are these people so cruel?
Little do you know, she suffers at school.
But all of the things anyone can hear,
Little do you know what flows in her ears
Would be your biggest fear.
Just stop all of your hate
Before it's too late.

Ruby Ava Canavan (11)
Cleethorpes Academy, Cleethorpes

Will Smith

What a legend he is
Back in the day, the Fresh Prince of Bel-Air
Where the day takes you to 1992
Bad Boys 1 and then Bad Boys 2
Independence Day and Wild Wild West
Also, he rapped sometimes, was the best
West Philadelphia, born and raised
Basketball was one of his favourite games
Still going strong to this day
Bad Boys for us now, on its way.

Harry Cook (11)
Cleethorpes Academy, Cleethorpes

The Future

Even though I am growing up
I just wanted to say...

Thank you, Mum
Thank you, Dad
For all the adventures we have had
Although me and Harry do fall out
he's still my flesh and blood,
love you all dearly.

Ellie Riley (11)
Cleethorpes Academy, Cleethorpes

Stop Bullying

Bullying is bad.
Bullying makes me feel sad.

Bullying is not nice
When you come around
I freeze like ice

You make me cry
And that's not alright.

Brooke Harniess (11)
Cleethorpes Academy, Cleethorpes

Quiet

People don't see me,
Or they don't look,
They find me,
The wolves, the hawks,
Eyeing me like their prey.

Ignore me is what I want them to do,
Leave me alone,
But they don't,
They never do.

Seeing the others,
Hearing them laugh,
They walk towards me.

They leap and pounce at me,
Hitting me and punching me,
Until I can't,
They do it because I can't stop them.

I'm gonna stop it,
I know I am,
One way or another,
The peace I will have,
I would pay anything for it,
And that,
Is what I will have.

Isobel Anne Lonergan (11)
Craigclowan Preparatory School, Perth

Polar Bears

P eople are highly endangering me as a polar bear!

O bviously, people are making it harder and worse.

L ots of us are dying because of icebergs!

A good friend of mine went swimming and never came back...

R ightfully, in 2020, we will take our revenge,

B y sending terribly, icy, snowy weather!

E very time someone drops a piece of litter, one of us dies.

A life for us polar bears can be very short,

R ough, sad, mean, cruel lives we have as polar bears,

S o glad me and my family are still alive today!

Islay Watson-Ross (11)
Craigclowan Preparatory School, Perth

Stop Poaching

When will they stop poaching for our tusks?
Every day, every minute and every second, non-stop!

We should not have to put up with this,
Elephants are going to be extinct!
They kill us for money,
Piano keys and carvings.

Every day, I have to move from home to home,
I've seen elephants die every day,
Just because of this problem.

I wish I could put my word out to the world and increase the
number of us.
I wish we had cameras and the news,
To show them what is happening to us,
So everyone could be more aware...

Lily MacNamara (11)
Craigclowan Preparatory School, Perth

Love Marmite

Stuck in an ice-cold room,
I heard thuds coming closer,
The lights flickered on and I could
See the huge world in front of me.
This hand reached for me,
I felt this feeling inside of me,
My heart began to pound...

But the hand just shoved me aside.
That feeling inside of me dropped suddenly,
The hand just came for the jam.
The door slammed shut and it
Plunged me into the darkness.
That feeling inside of me just
Got flushed away.
Sadness rushed inside of me.
Why do people never choose me
For their toast?

Luisa Alexander (11)
Craigclowan Preparatory School, Perth

Surviving Cancer

I slowly opened my eyes,
My heart beating and quickening,
I was free from the burden,
Finally, my scenery of normal hospital walls,
Turned into rows of hills and trees.

The car was driving for quite a while,
My life had turned from sudden death,
To being free and living the rest of my life.

Suddenly, we stopped,
I had arrived at the tall building, my house,
My heart was beating, my tummy churning,
My family ran out into the garden,
Hugging and greeting me.

I was home at last.

Aoife Jordan (11)
Craigclowan Preparatory School, Perth

Fame And Shame

Walking anxiously onto the stage,
Hearing the crowd roar,
And the paparazzi's cameras click.

Suddenly, all the boiling lights
Were on me, shining bright!
I felt the sweat rolling down my skin,
And the pressure turned on.

My stomach started to move,
Spin, turn and churn,
And then I felt it come up and out.

All I felt was shame and anxiety,
All I heard was booing and a ringing in my ear,
All I saw was a blur and then, suddenly, darkness...

Bo Macdonald (12)
Craigclowan Preparatory School, Perth

Alone

I sat silently alone,
I was travelling to the unknown.
I was miserable,
Deep in thought.
I sat uncomfortably,
Still alone.

Out of the hundreds,
There was nobody,
Nobody,
Who wanted to speak,
Or even look at me.

Alone.
Still alone.

I was dying inside,
Crying so loud,
My mother could probably hear.

Alone.
Still alone.

Anna Isabella Hope (11)
Craigclowan Preparatory School, Perth

Animal Cruelty

Stuck staring at the beast,
trying to figure out why
and what was happening to this world.

Why would they have such a big whip
or have it in a cage so small?

But it's not just this animal.

Everywhere I look,
I see animals that have been enslaved
and trained so cruelly.
I stare...

Neve Weir (11)
Craigclowan Preparatory School, Perth

Sofie Dossi

S uper flexible
O ver-bendy
F lexibility and fantastic flips are my thing
I stretch every day
E ven when I am tired

D oing contortions is fun
O xygen is key
S o flexible, that's me
S ofie Dossi is me
I am going to have a flex.

Emily Laird (11)
Craigclowan Preparatory School, Perth

Traffic Light

Red, amber, green,
That's all I do,
And it's all for you.

I'm asleep,
They press a button,
It wakes me up,
And then I change.

These big coloured things,
Come charging towards me,
They slow and they stop,
And wait for me.

The people are waiting,
So I let them go,
And the cars sit there,
Getting frustrated and ready to go.

So I start all over again,
Going green, amber, red,
Then people cross,
And the cars go again.

Isla Smith (11)
Dalkeith High School, Dalkeith

A Tree

A seed in a packet
A sapling in the ground
I grew and I grew
Until I was the tallest in the woods

Life was boring
Life was plain
Until one day when a little girl came
She looked up in awe
And called for her dad

Over the weeks
And over the months
The house in my branches began to appear
They came every day to hammer and saw
Then one day, at the breaking of dawn
The girl climbed the ladder with her family cheering her on

She came every day
Sometimes with friends
And they would play

But on one summer day
She never came
I waited for years
With the house that was decaying

Then one tragic day
In the thunder and the rain
Lightning hit me
And I fell to the floor...

Amy Robb (11)
Dalkeith High School, Dalkeith

Journey

I get used once,
I get thrown away.
I land on the ground,
and get blown away.

I land in the ocean,
I float about for days,
I get eaten by a turtle,
who thinks I am food.
I suffocate the turtle.

I get washed up on a beach,
I get picked up by people,
I get put in a bin,
and sent to be recycled.

Thomas Roy (12)
Dalkeith High School, Dalkeith

An Extraterrestrial Opinion

Disguised as some 'space junk', I've orbited the Earth
Hidden in plain sight long since my birth
Observing the planet from a very young age
It's time to express my thoughts on this page

Earth is a beautiful place I conclude
But the Earthlings, I don't get why they are so rude!
They judge each other based on traits like 'skin colour' or 'gender'
Their courts often fail to punish a serious offender

They are destroying the planet, though the pace may be slow
Those powerful feign ignorance or pretend not to know
Young humans petition, asking for a change in their ways
Yet lack of action is hidden by an outpouring of praise

They insult each other daily and just do as they please
Hurling insults like trash and names such as these
There's pain from these actions more than some tend to show
But bullying continues, they ignore 'stop' and 'no'

If you are reading this, please do not go to Earth
Their lack of tolerance for foreigners diminishes its worth
The environment is hostile and being destroyed by the minute
And respect is given, you must work overtime to kill it.

Alyssa Baines (13)
Dereham Neatherd High School, Dereham

What About Me?

My face is littered with your scars,
Every second, you cut them deeper,
Air is all around me but I can't breathe,
I know I belong here but I want to leave.

Water, earth, wind and fire,
My origins and my end,
Something's destroying my figure,
Something much, much bigger.

Hate is a strong word,
Linked to enemy and grudge,
Something I have never expressed,
But describes something I absolutely detest.

Sometimes they forget I'm even here,
Forget my feelings and emotions,
Well, I have something to say,
"At this rate, I'll have to forget you one day!"

Because, I am your Planet Earth,
I've cared for you since birth,
But, how have you repaid me?
You haven't, you've betrayed me.

Dali Sophia Brady (12)
Dereham Neatherd High School, Dereham

Blitz

Boots stomping, the soles of despair
The outbreak of war - so unfair.
A march to a battlefield,
So full of hate.
And an ever-increasing death-rate.

A bang, then a scream,
The beginning of a bad dream.
When death came marching by,
And stifling sounds of war,
Came a horrible sight I saw.

Bodies littered the beach,
And to God, I beseech.
For to my mind came a dreadful thought.
That soon I would see the gates of Heaven,
And life - now filled with depression.

But I didn't let that stop me:
Instead, it inspired me.
I knew I had the power,
So whilst I can shout,
I let it all out.

But the Devil had a sight on me,
And so I paid a deadly fee;
I had sold my life away.

So I fell and stared at the sky,
As happy thoughts came shipping by.

Sam Goward (11)
Dereham Neatherd High School, Dereham

I Don't Want To Talk

I don't want to talk,
Some will stare and some will laugh,
I accept that I look different
And I pity you because you are all the same.
I don't want to talk,
I watch you play, eat and laugh together
Whilst I curl up in my cave of shame,
How I wish I had a shoulder to cry on,
I don't want to talk.
I tried... and tried... and tried...
But you will always just run away.
Are friends really so hard to capture?

I think I need to talk,
You will call me ugly, fat, dumb or a loner,
I hope, someday, you will realise that I have feelings
Because I am actually no different to you.
I think I need to talk,
It's time for you to imagine what I witness,
Take the shard out of my heart and include me,
Because, we're the same, you and me,
It is time to talk.
Reluctantly, I speak with my smarmy nemesis,
With resilience and courage, I retreat from the cave,
I feel happier and stronger than I ever felt before,
So, I will advise you, when you're feeling down,
Just talk.

Nathaniel James Turner (13)
Dover College, Dover

Black, White

Black, white, black, white,
This is all I can see,
The occasional magpie lurking behind whispering trees,
But, I know I can see further,
A rainbow of colours...
But, surely, this isn't allowed because
I am simply among the others
Who are blindsided to the colour cascading around them,
Only focusing on one, insignificant thing that is fueling other sorrows.
Crazy, crazy, crazy, circling their heads,
Don't look because maybe, just maybe,
If we ignore it, all the colours will go away
Until all that is left is
Black, white, black, white...

Belle Klappa (14)

Dover College, Dover

Spin, Spin, Spin

I am made of stainless steel,
Titanium and copper,
You spin me right round,
Right round like you never have,
I typically have two or three
Flat structures next to me,
By my side,
I am bought by ten-year-olds
Who usually have really greasy
And disgusting fingers
And, then, every now and then,
I get traded and end up
Having more and more bacteria on me,
Sometimes, people even take out my heart
And then put it back,
But every time they do that,
It makes me spin slower.

August Moos (13)
Dover College, Dover

Bullied Ball

I am calm and excited, if that makes sense,
The feeling of grass against me,
The way the damp, green fingers run through my black and
white hair,
Tense as I see the bullies launching themselves closer and
closer at me
Until I get kicked all the way into the big spiderweb.
Although, when the day comes to an end,
I am hurt, bruised and my feelings are crushed,
Now, I am okay, knowing my best friend is blowing me up,
Now, I am just waiting for it to happen once again.

Avy Taylor (13)
Dover College, Dover

The Winston Churchill Rap

My name is Winston, ends with a Churchill,
I was Prime Minister in World War Two
And the Nazis once I killed,
They were very ill,
Many died from disease,
They weren't very pleased,
What happened to them?
They were chucking up phlegm,
They got put down,
Now, they're under the ground.
World War Two came to an end,
The Germans will never attend,
God bless the heroes,
You will never be a zero.

Samuel James Smith (13)
Dover College, Dover

Marmite

From people, I can have love and I can have hate,
I have a lot more salt in me than a slice of cake,
Spread me on toast any time of the day
But never waste me by throwing me away.
I am like thick, black marsh in a jar,
I can also be like a twin of tar.
Once you eat me, I'm sure you'll feel great,
Then you can be my best mate,
Eat me and love me without making me sad.

Scarlett Rathmell (13)
Dover College, Dover

The Sun

In the morning, I rise,
At night, I sink,
I light up the day,
But I am tired at the end,
But, I have to do my job
And there's no other way,
I'm a yellow ball of fire,
I am very hot.

Rishma Patel (13)
Dover College, Dover

Fame

There are consequences for having fame,
I reached for the stars but, very soon,
I noticed there are consequences for having fame.

Sometimes, I want to go out in my pyjamas with a bag of crisps,
But that thought got thrown away because of all the fans and paparazzi.

My face is my biggest asset
And ageing is my biggest fear.

Being famous is like being in a zoo,
You can never escape the staring eyes, glaring at you.

Are these friends here for my company?
Or are they just here for the money that accompanies me?

I hear lies about me everywhere
And I think to myself that is not me,
That's someone
That someone has built me up to be.

If only I could have a second alone,
I would drink tea unaccompanied at my home.

Isabel Bird (13)
Greenfields School, Forest Row

The Living Kingdom

The animals, the mammals, the reptiles that used to reside,
The roar of the dinosaurs and the reaping growl of the
bears,
The monkey that swings from vine to vine,
The tiger that leaps to meet his holy shrine,
The giraffe that sets foot on the mighty, gold plain,
With the sunset going down, mosquitos chewing sugar cane,
The wolf on the mountain peak,
The little bird's baby squeak,
There is the sun shining on the bursting, peach horizon,
Following behind
A pride in a dozen.

Reese Elan Wilson (12)
Greenfields School, Forest Row

The Messages

I opened my phone, scared about what I might see,
The dreadful messages staring up at me,
I read them all, they wouldn't stray,
Scrolling through...
I stared and stared wishing they would go away!
They felt like they were here to stay,
As I read the messages, I felt tears in my eyes,
Why? Why me? I was taken by surprise,
I didn't know what to do, or who to turn to,
My family, my friends, they wouldn't understand,
I was alone...

Porscha Smith (12)
Greenfields School, Forest Row

The King Of The Jungle

I am hanging in the trees,
Benefitting the fresh breeze
And, all of a sudden, I sniff the smell of a blue baboon!
He opens up his golden banana,
He drops the glimmering pome,
I look at him... He looks at me,
I swing freely from the eucalyptus tree,
While he slips, I dip down and the glorious drupe,
As the Chacma is tangled in the vines,
Watching me eat the brilliant produce.
I am now the King of the Jungle.

Sophia Garcia (13)
Greenfields School, Forest Row

The Animal Kingdom

I am a cub, a lion cub,
My dad is big and brave,
His roar echoes through the land,
One day his roar was silent.

Now he hangs on a wall just for pride,
But not *his* pride,
There is a shotgun on the floor.

My dad's roar will go on,
Not from him
But through his son.

Lulu Gabriella Borg (14)
Greenfields School, Forest Row

Gunshots

I heard gunshots,
Hiding in the place my dad told me to sit,
Sitting there, praying to God not to be spotted,
Thinking of all these weeks and the conflicts,
The way my mother did plaits in my hair,
Is something that will never be forgotten,
Doing braids in my hair so I would not be killed,
Doing this because I am a Sikh boy,
Slowly, but quickly, in my eyes, tears were filled,
In these few weeks, it felt like happiness was over,
We were never going to be in joy,
Frightened that I will never see my family again,
I cautiously look up,
Trying to see my parents or anybody but all I can see are
men,
Men armed with guns,
I need to find my parents so I quickly jump,
Millions of thoughts crossing my mind,
Seeing these dead people on the floor,
Innocent people dead,
I look around, all I see are dead people,
There is nobody here except military men
Standing there, watching the dead.
I heard gunshots.

Parjot Sandhu (13)
Heston Community School, Heston

Water, Water Everywhere

I have been there since the beginning of man,
Might still be there by the end of man,
Moving with the flow of the world,
Essential to young and old,
Oh, what can you do without me?

Home to water rats, pirates, I mean,
Home to water travellers, sailors, I mean,
Many have fallen into my cold embrace, so unfortunate
And many are still trapped in my dark depths to date,
Oh, what can you do without me?

Cold, hot, warm, you get me in different ways,
Dirty, clean, muddy, you get me in different ways,
Different diseases in me are passed,
Different memories and goodness in me is passed,
Oh, what can you do without me?

In daylight, you see most of my might,
But you see calm low tide at night,
Hugest of living creatures in my depth,
Hiding little ones in my dark as they crept,
Oh, what can you do without me?

Hot sun soaks me up, there goes evaporation,
Cooling down into a soft, cloudy bed, there goes
condensation,
And, oh well, down I go to wet everything, there goes
precipitation,

Snow? Hail? Rain? All are still precipitation
And the cycle goes on and on and on.

Omolara Zainab Moloney (13)
Heston Community School, Heston

The Fear Of Being The King Of The Jungle!

I am the king of the jungle,
So hungry and thirsty to strangle,
But what to do if my nature is to eat and kill,
I have no choice to go against my will.

As I roar as loud as thunder,
The families start to asunder,
They call me the king, yet I wear no crown,
But, all I do is sit by myself and frown.

They are frightened so badly,
Yet, they don't know I am so lonely,
I admit I fall into anger,
But, only because they fear that they are in danger.

I am supposed to be called the king because I am here to protect,
But, who am I a king for if they don't feel safe?
They judge me by my innocence,
All I'm trying to do is make friends.

Thinking they will get kidnapped,
They don't know it's not a trap,
This is a letter to you, all my lovely animals,
Will you all be my friends?
I'm the king of the jungle!

Dhruv Kirtesh Shah (13)
Heston Community School, Heston

I Have A Say About Something!

I have a say about something,
Something you all know about,
Something that you are taking away from yourself.

I have a say about something,
I have been here for more than you can ever think,
I help you live in this world you have created,
You are taking that privilege away from you,
You are destroying my friends' homes
By taking me away from you.

I have a say about something,
The fumes you have created
Helps me, not you,
You're destroying your own life
By taking me away from you.

I have a say about something,
Just because I'm silent, doesn't mean I can't hear you,
You're destroying oncoming futures which you're not going
to be here for
By taking me away from you.

I have a say about something,
Something you all know about,
Something that you are taking away from yourself.

Nancy Sunil Dutt (13)
Heston Community School, Heston

Delicious Doughnut

Hi, my name is Krispy Kreme
And I'm probably your best dream,
I could make you laugh with so much joy,
The last thing I want you to do is treat me like a toy,
I come in all flavours and sizes,
Plus, I'm full of surprises.

I'm mostly eaten in the middle of the night,
They munch me down with their biggest bites,
Maybe so with cinnamon and icing white,
Sure tempts other people, alright!

You can buy me in different shops,
Next to the ice cream section and lollipops,
I am surely no joke,
I even put a smile on the most modest of blokes,
Blows their tastebuds away,
Then come to buy me nearly every day,
Come in,
I have caramel, chocolate and lemon meringue pie,
Now the markets are getting undersupplied
Due to the demand, which is so high!

Karanveer Sondh (13)
Heston Community School, Heston

On The Come Up!

My father was killed,
Oh, why did this happen?
It brought me to tears.
After then, my mum was hooked on drugs,
She started pouring toxic into my ears.

I. Got. In.
Everyone is saying rapping should go in the bin,
Battling in the ring is my dream,
For everyone including you, him and me.

Battling in the ring against this thing
Who's chatting about my father,
If I was him, I wouldn't even bother
Because all I said is, "Your mother!"

Racism around the hood
Got thrown on the ground
'Cause 'I'm no good',
Pin me to the ground,
Boy you messed up,
Wrote me off,
Called your squad but you lucked up,
If I did what I wanted and tucked up,
You'd be bound for the ground,
Grave dug up.

Taysier Sami (12)
Heston Community School, Heston

A Childhood I'd Never Forget

At the age of thirteen, it all changed, I went into care,
I was scared and shocked about what was happening,
All I had seen was me, being taken away from my family,
I went to live with foster parents and lived without my
sisters.

I lived with these carers for one year, it was hard to
understand,
We all had to keep such a big secret from family,
A few months later, I went back home with my sisters, I was
happy,
But, after a few months, things deteriorated, I went back
into care
But, without my sisters.

After a while, I went home for good, on my own, without my
sisters,
I was happy to be home but unhappy, my sisters were no
longer with me,
I am now much older and I understand why I was taken
away,
Life changed for the better!

Gursimran Kaur Chouhan (12)
Heston Community School, Heston

We Lived In Hiding For Two Years

My family and five more people
Went into hiding in
A small apartment
Which I referred to as the Secret Annex,
We lived in constant fear
Of being discovered and
Could never go outside.
We remained silent during
Daytime in order to avoid suspicion
To the people who were working
In the warehouse below us.
I tasted bland beans and vegetables
For two years,
I wished that we could be free,
I thought about how independent I was becoming,
When I grow up, I wanted to be
An author or a journalist,
I wanted to publish my diary
About how I lived in the Secret Annex,
With eight people (me included)
And how life was.

Adeline Sam (13)
Heston Community School, Heston

Stuck

The pain inside me,
Alone, with no one beside me,
The anger burns my skin
When I'm reminded of my past.

But, it all happened so fast.

My fingers wrap around my thin wrist,
My pale legs,
Numb.
My fingernails filled with grime,
Crooked, reaching to an inch,
People see me as a nasty witch.

I wish I could have the chance to go out
And show the world murder is not what I'm all about,
I have no idea how long I've been here,
But it feels like infinity,
I'm not the person I'm painted out to be,
My only hope is to be set free.

Imaan Akhtar (13)
Heston Community School, Heston

My Hair

Why am I so wavy?
Why am I so slick?
Why am I so sexy?
Why am I so thick?

People look at me and their mouth waters,
Yes, I'm amazing,
Yes, I'm impeccable,
I got people dazing,
They say it's respectable.

I'm the best you'll ever see
And, trust me, you won't disagree,
I'm smooth, I'm wavy,
I got certain people going all crazy.

I look so good when I'm wet,
I look so good when I'm dry
And if I say I'm not the best,
Everyone will say that's a lie.

Yunis Haider (13)
Heston Community School, Heston

Fear

The plane flew day and night,
No one came to save us,
People were murdered day by day,
Still, no one came to save us.

They struck the passengers with fear and fright,
No one came to save us,
Cries went off day by day,
Still, no one came to save us.

They threatened to kill me,
No one came to save us,
I held both of my hands tightly,
Still, no one came to save us.

No one came to save us,
This is no joke, no child's play,
These people once lived happily,
Now live in fear.

Herneet Kaur Gaba (12)
Heston Community School, Heston

Merciless Matilda Enters Her Doom!

Full of nails,
Full of darts,
Full of everything that's sharp,
Merciless Matilda enters her doom!

Trunchbull locks her drawer,
She wants to be cruel even more,
She needs a stop and be given a cure,
Merciless Matilda enters her doom!

Olympic star should be behind bars,
Getting cheated of a car,
Then chases the dad far,
Merciless Matilda enters her doom!

For this, Matilda becomes the aim,
For this, Matilda was in shame,
For this, her dad was to blame,
Merciless Matilda enters her doom!

Jasmeen Kaur (12)
Heston Community School, Heston

Fearless

King of the jungle is what I'm known for,
For my family, I will start a war,
Fearless and fierce is my roar,
Loud and rustling from its core.

Fearless is realness.

Being the toughest is my law,
Once you're fearless, there is no play,
Enemies, prey, predators too,
They will run and I will pursue.

Realness is fearless.

I will fight alone, though I am never alone,
You look at me and see nothing but stone
As I am the king with my throne.

I am fearless.

Arjan Athwal (13)
Heston Community School, Heston

Two Lives

I made my way into
A warm atmosphere,
I made my way up to
A cosy corner,
I attempted to spin
A web,
I got myself ready
To catch my prey.

I suddenly saw
A big, black shadow,
It got bigger, bigger
And bigger,
Until I heard
The smack of a firework,

I fell asleep
As I heard a sweep,
I woke up
And heard a cup,
My eyes opened,
I felt broken,
I was at the same place
And left no trace.

Gabriela Ujma (13)
Heston Community School, Heston

Charlie And The Chocolate Bar

Everyone is surrounded by the desire to get a chocolate bar,
If only I could have one, I would share
With my family as we admired the stars
Shining above us, high in the air,
I would really love this treat,
As today is my birthday!
But, my family do not have much to eat,
We need a lot to pay
For a chocolate bar we will finish in a week,
As I arrive home, my mother is standing in the doorway,
She shows me my treat
And we go inside and eat.

Octavio Pinto (13)
Heston Community School, Heston

The Newborn Crocodile

On the bank of the Amazon river,
Born from a giant egg,
I gave a good shiver
And stood on my green legs.

My very first swim,
I swam around a log,
My tail looked prim
And I befriended a frog.

I caught my first fish
So I could eat a dish,
I had to hold ground
So I didn't lose grip.

I grow older by the day
And I catch my own prey,
I wish to still travel,
To explore the Amazon marvel.

Dylan Afonso (13)
Heston Community School, Heston

My Best Friend

A pretty, magical creature
With stunning blue eyes,
Her horn shimmering
In the pale moonlight,
She trotted majestically towards me
Through the enchanted forest,
Her soft, smooth mane
Brushed against my hair,
I felt a warmth of joy
Throughout my body,
She knelt her head down
And nuzzled the side of my face,
From that moment on,
I knew we would be best friends forever.

Navdeep Kaur Kharay (12)
Heston Community School, Heston

Teardrops

A drop of a person's soul,
Cascading down through unwanted tears
As the words run straight into his ears,
A buoyant heart,
Torn apart,
A smile transformed to knitted brows,
His world has turned upside down,
If you've never had any tears to shed,
Beware they may fall in the days that lie ahead.

Pakeeza Siddiqui (13)
Heston Community School, Heston

I Dreamed Tonight

I ran upstairs,
I turned off the lights,
I went to bed
And I dreamed tonight.

I saw a balloon,
I held onto the balloon
And I flew to the moon.

I played on the moon,
I danced on the moon,
I slept on the moon
And I woke up in the afternoon.

Pavleen Madhan (12)
Heston Community School, Heston

Her?

Her small ballet shoes,
Her short, plastic legs,
Her slim, flat body,
Her plastic arms,
Her two, strong shoulders,
Her rose-red lips,
Her chubby, plastic cheeks,
Her dull, black eyes,
Her sharp, red hair,
Do you know her
Or does she know you?

Aamna Ali (13)
Heston Community School, Heston

A Night In The Life

I sip on the cold night air,
The invisible smoke weaving through my teeth.
Linked, arm-in-arm, by striding gateposts,
(Joey and Sam could tower over the entire world!)

I told my parents a lie you see,
Fragile shields that cage me from the outside world.
The world that holds such evil things as:
Sex, drugs and boys!

Their bones as thin as paper,
Quaking at the mere thought of me even breathing
The air that lies behind the front door.

They ask, "Wh-what are you doing?"
Faint, they might as well have done!
"Lyndsey invited me over."
Not a total lie, I am with Lyndsey, present... well...

"Oh good! She's sensible."
That's their word for a virgin.

I look back,
The distant echo of my parents' timid voices shouting,
"Remember, no boys!" as I slam the door shaking my head,
laughing.
My drunken beam fades to rain.
I take them for granted.

You should apologise
I can't understand why you despise
Their tender love and affection
To turn and walk the other direction.
Oh shut up!
Stop giving me grief!

She cried through grinding teeth.

I'm going to ignore you now.

Oh wow
Not like you haven't done that before.

Hm. Wait, I see it! The rainbow lights!
Shining red, blue, pink, green.
A spiral of pure joy mixed with teen rebellion.
An ecstasy of adolescence.
(If you catch my drift.)

"Sally!" Joey and Sam pull me back
As I, unexpectedly, fall to the sharp, unforgiving concrete.
I see Suki next to me.

It's her crush.
She had been Sherlocking him all term.
Sticking fragments of them
(Polaroid photos of the two)
On her faded pink wall. Ugh!

Saying that about your friend!
"We will be together, till the end!"
You said to her, well you lied.

I didn't mean it!

She cried again!
They're staring at you know, your 'friends'.
And you dare interrupt me!
You asylum freak to be!

Right! That's it! I'm shutting you off!
With the soothing and knowledgable distraction,
Of a conversation with Jamie!

Where she got the idea
That I wanted an argument is unbeknownst to me!
But I'm ready for the cold, colourful kick of a drink.

I look down at the drinks' table,
Seeing a city of beverages before me.
Beer, v-vodka... punch bowl?
She has a punch bowl?

She has a punch bowl.

Although, I'm not at the stage where things get crazy.

And your vision gets a little hazy...

I'll skip the punch bowl
And get right to the gut!

A fancy Caribbean beer, m'lady?
Why, don't mind if I do!

Where are we again, remind me.
There are some dodgy people behind me.

Oh! So, you've decided to calm down, eh?
You like to do that.

What, take a chill pill?
I'm not ill!

No, as soon as I continue to describe
The bohemian scene in front of me,
You become a joker,
Playing a trick on me.
Well, I won't fall for it.

Okay, okay! I'll be quiet.
No need to start a riot.

Hmm... I need to find someone
To let my thoughts become
A physical manifestation through words.
Simple, plain conversation.

But Jamie is off snogging someone.
It's so interesting how all these people
Have so many identities.

Everyone is different, that's true
But I'm feeling blue.

Why?

Because we're leaving now.

What? Oh wow, I must've blacked out.
I got real drunk.

I'm collecting my things, fortunately I have everything.
(Phone, purse, keys, bag.)
The daylight pours through the window
Rippling in between the hungover rubble on the floor.
I open the front door, looking back,
Thinking about this
Night in the life.

Eddie Thomas (15)
Kingsmead School, Hoylake

Figs And Orange Blossom

Figs and orange blossom
Are the antithesis of war.

Bustling markets and warm aromas, scented meat encased
in grape leaves, mint, garlic and turmeric
Irate gunfire, land scorched with revulsion,
Replace plump pomegranates.

Horizons curtailed by shards of glass, spikes of metal, smoke
helix,
All the meltdown of humanity.

Children narrow and strain eyes, yearning for safety,
Just any place, any pocket of air - not contaminated and
where the tyrant of war cannot reach them,
The planes departed for warm beaches, relaxed
destinations,
But they now deposit maiming bombs and burning
chemicals.
Survivors confined to a limited space providing little shelter,
the malaise all around them.

A solitary tree stands amongst the havoc, leaves growing
the compost of hope,
A symbol of the future.

Jack Oliver Hall (11)
Kingsmead School, Hoylake

Tonight And Tomorrow

Between tonight and tomorrow,
A silent voice will cease to exist,
Unbeknownst to us, whether you realise it or not,
Another will soon follow,
So wake up from your blissful dream
And look,
Open your eyes and look, there's a whole world out there,
Do not let more erase themselves,
All it takes is one person
So let that one person be you
And stop these lights from going out.
Between tonight and tomorrow,
No more will cease to exist,
All will be cherished
Between tonight and tomorrow.

Between yesterday and this morning,
A light lit up.
Between today and tonight,
A smile appeared.
Between tonight and tomorrow,
The light will go out.
Between today and five years from now,
They will still go out.
Silent screams echoing in dreams,
Cries lost between the stars,
Between tonight and tomorrow,

How many will we forget?
Between tonight and tomorrow,
How many can we save?

Anusha Tahir (15)
Loxford School, Ilford

The Opposite Of Love

These days,
Love is defined by
Illuminated screens
And a tendency to be mean,
A memory that never left me,
How can I ever be free?

A connection
As unsteady as my Wi-Fi signal,
Yet there's no communication,
Frustration
The indentations etched on my heart,
Some may say is a work of art.

When did love turn to
Hate?
Those we once knew strangers,
Hearts unaware of the dangers,
Holding onto comfort
Whilst feelings uncovered are hurt.

Brackish tears
Engulf and radiate my eyes,
Reflecting the cyan light,
Streaming down my face; lost the fight,
The hate consumes my sanity,
How can I find clarity?

The opposite of love is not hate
Ignorant people behind pixels,
Keyboard warriors
They couldn't be sorrier
For the pain in their words,
Commenting all things absurd.

The opposite of love is not hate.

Amanjit Singh (15)
Loxford School, Ilford

Begin With Love

Begin with love, forever to the end,
A simple word which we often send.

A heart full of love
Pumps to every beat
To whom it ever meets.

A work done with love is priceless and appreciated,
A work done without is cheap and often hated.

Love has no colour, faith or race,
No limits, no borders and needs no space.

Still, we test it every day by words and gifts,
Broken and brought, they do not last,
For the true price of love is love itself.

Sincere, true love is never bought and sold,
Its price is worth more than gold,
Love is so beautiful in nature and life
Resembled by the heart,
I cannot be torn apart.

Love always wins, fighting the hate we hold within,
Lives are lost, scars remain,
Let's make peace with love, with whatever time remains.
Begin with love, forever to the end,
A simple word which we should all send.

Alisha Gulrez
Loxford School, Ilford

Already A Hero

If he dies in the warzone tomorrow,
Nothing will be heard, except his sorrow,
Placing his medals on his chest,
Showing his mum he did his best,
Hearing all the screams and seeing all the tears,
Yet, he will fight death despite his fears,
His country comes first above this all.
He needs to prove himself before his fall,
Something has to be done within this hour
Before death catches him and replaces him with a flower,
Hoping, in the end, there will be a ray of light,
However, the next day came, and he wasn't in sight,
All those cherished memories dispersed from his head,
Looking back in his room laid an empty bed,
Every day, staring at the scars that remained on his bone,
His dad once shot him in the heart by saying,
"You will always be a zero,"
But, the thought of him being laid dead,
Instead of others,
Proved he was already a hero.

Simran Patti
Loxford School, Ilford

Death Row

19.02.1904 - My last day...

Dear World,
Here I am
Standing, alone,
Where is the world?
When is my future?

Here I stand
Away from home,
Trapped between these walls
Whilst battling my griefs and moans.

The words still echoed in my mind,
The feeling took me back in time,
The darkness had closed in on me,
Now they'll take away what is rightfully mine.
Her screams,
They still haunt me,
Her blood,
It still taunts me.

The weapon that was never mine
Had turned on me that one, cruel time.

Now, I will have to suffer,
Now, I must feel the pain,
Once that needle pricks me,
They may strike back, once again.

But, before I go away,
There is one thing you must know,
It was never me,
It was never, ever me.

Farewell...

Erica Hossain
Loxford School, Ilford

Beginning's End

There's nothing I can say or do
This is destiny in truth.

Your love for me was so warm,
But your love for others is so torn,
I'm still holding onto that afternoon
So, won't you come back soon?

You lived those nights without care
While we laughed about the future,
Now we are no longer the perfect pair,
Inseparable! But you became the creature.

So, I guess in the scheme of things,
I'm not the only one
Now knowing there's so much more to life
Than living just for fun.

Now, every time you kill me,
I am born again,
Every time you say you love me,
I act like I don't care.
Every new beginning,
Comes from some beginning's end.

Sophie Davouloury (15)
Loxford School, Ilford

A Bond Stronger Than Blood

A smile we all share in common,
A silent tear only we know,
A bond stronger than blood.

Arms that would hug me tight
After I had cried all night,
The only comfort I needed was her.

Her eyes gleamed with joy
As he played with his newly-bought toy,
We watched him play all day.

She looked proudly at her work,
Knowing, together, they had great teamwork
And that, one day, it will be a memory through time.

She laughed at his goofy smile
As she hugged him for a while,
Not wanting to ever let go.

She looked back at the memories
With a smile only we can see,
A tear only we know,
A family made, not by blood, but love.

Iman Nasir (15)
Loxford School, Ilford

Anne Frank - Hidden

Hidden.
Lost.
Scared.
Imagine hiding for most of your life,
You can't, right?
Not walking around on the streets,
Just like a prisoner,
However, I did not commit any crimes,
You must hear these words from each criminal,
But, ask a criminal,
"Are you in prison because of your religion?"
Ask a criminal,
"Are you in prison because of your ethnicity?"
Ask a criminal,
"Can you be a prisoner even if you're not in prison?"
Yes, a prisoner,
Not able to have any freedom,
Hiding from the actual criminals,
To Hitler, I'm just
Hidden.
Lost.
Scared.

Amandeep Manku (16)
Loxford School, Ilford

Adversity

The constant, overwhelming fear of being wrong
Making me feel like I don't belong,
In this desolate land, abandoned by two of my kind
Who loaded my heart with happiness and desire
To live my life deemed prior,
To achieve everyone's approval,
To live my life how I acquire.

The thought of a life so ideal and complete,
Where we don't have to be told
To suppress the bold and daring thoughts
That circulate through your mind,
Wanting to defy the mastermind
Behind lies confined,
Spiral, spinning endlessly in a cycle
Of repeated products of this world's adversity.

Aisha Ahmed (15)
Loxford School, Ilford

The Jaws Of Joy

Oh, how much we all hate school,
It's boring, it's frustrating, it's hard,
How we all wish for school to end,
It's long, it's exhausting, it's tiring,
We all just want to escape the jaws of hell.

But, then, we begin to say,

Oh, how much we all loved school,
It was fun, it was interesting, it was cool,
How we all wished for school to continue,
It was amazing, it was lovely, it was great,
We all just want to go back to the jaws of joy.

Zainab Hamid
Loxford School, Ilford

Fifteen

Fifteen,
They say we're mean,
We get into fights and try not to scream,
We really aren't too keen
But, behind this face, like a screen,
Is a scared, little teen.

Fifteen,
We're in between,
Trying to get our lives together
'Cause we can't all be queens,
To get somewhere our brains
Have to work like machines,
We'll never be supreme
'Cause we're fifteen.

Eesha Nadeem (15)
Loxford School, Ilford

What It's Like Being A Teen

T ough on the outside, soft on the inside,
E very day, hanging outside,
E njoying their company from a friend,
N ever wishing for the fun to end,
A geing year by year,
G etting into adulthood, trying not to be full of fear,
E xiting their teenage years to be understood.

Amaya Ruckmal
Loxford School, Ilford

A Soldier's Heart

A heart full of gold,
Always warm, never cold,
They never leave a man behind
As they put their lives after mankind,
Fighting wars and being in danger
Will lead to tears falling from strangers,
A soldier's heart is never cold.

Tafanique Service
Loxford School, Ilford

Fighter Of Death

(As J.K. Rowling)

I had no sense, mind, heart or eyes,
I had no life.

College left me,
Mother left me,
My child left me.

He shouted,
I shouted,
he screamed,
I screamed
'til I screamed and shouted no more,
'til I saw his face no more.

Tiny house,
tiny life,
single mum,
jobless,
penniless,
poor with a home.

It's true,
I wanted to see my blood run
through my fingers,
I wanted to see my blood trickle,
I saw no light.

Cafe, hotel, house, room, rented home,
I wrote, I wrote,
rejected more than a dozen,
accepted by one
and, then,
author of the year.

Here I am,
snitches, bludgers and beaters through my head
but I still stay strong.
Death gave me many chances
and
I held on. Tightly.

Now, people scream my name,
now, people know my name,
now, people hear my name,
now, I am proud of my name.

So, don't cry,
don't keep it inside,
let it out,
people will know your name,
a fighter of death.

Aren't we all frightened of death?

Safiyyah Islam (12)
Madani Girls' School, Whitechapel

Stand Back Up

Life isn't just about gaining success,
It's about learning lessons, more or less,
You need to learn how to bounce back up again
And not let failure hold you down like a chain.

We all have goals and dreams
And things we want to achieve,
But, we must always remember
That failure will always be out there
And to fight it is the best thing ever
Because

Life isn't just about gaining success,
It's about learning lessons, more or less,
You need to learn how to bounce back up again
And not let failure hold you down like a chain.

To be successful, you must have knowledge and do your
part,
But to fight failure, you need to be strong, both in your mind
and your heart,
Failure may be the only thing people see
But that is not who you are supposed to be,
It's hard work that gets you back up again,
So never give up, no matter how hard the pain.

Abida Ahmed (12)
Madani Girls' School, Whitechapel

Nelson Mandela

As a child, he dreamt of changing his country,
Who knew he would be in jail for two centuries?
As he grew, he dreamt of South Africa, where no one would oppress,
That would have been best,
As a man, he changed everything,
Who knew freedom was what he could bring?

Equality was his aim!

A man of peace who fought our fight,
Just so we could have our rights.
Personified kindness and embodied humility,
Just so we can be free.
Surviving in that cell for years,
Just so we can overcome our fears.
Fought out wars and battles,
Just so we can settle.

Equality was his aim!

As the sun meets the horizon,
We bid you farewell,
You had an amazing story to tell.

Jannat Basith (12)
Madani Girls' School, Whitechapel

Fear

Invisible, yet everyone feels you,
Silent, yet everyone hears you,
Making and breaking,
Swift and efficient,
Everyone's afraid of you,
Afraid to accept you,
That doesn't matter,
You invade them,
Thoughts, emotions,
They cower at the sight of you,
So misunderstood
They don't see
That you make them human,
You make them
But you can break them,
Hovering over people,
Drifting around silently
But you're there,
Always there,
You're everywhere
And they know it,
They're so afraid to speak,
They beg you for a way out,
Scared of what you show them
But, sometimes, they overcome you,
Make you scared.

No matter,
For you'll always find your way back to them,
You're so powerful yet you can be weak,
But, who are you,
You're fear.

Samiyyah Najiba (13)
Madani Girls' School, Whitechapel

In The Trenches

All through the night, the bombs are loud,
And I am filled with dread.
Despite my exhaustion, I'm wide awake,
But that other guy is dead.

Though the gunshots do not let me sleep,
I dream of life back home.
My mother's soup, my safe warm bed,
The girl I call my own.

Home,
It will be there.
Home,
I will get there.

Erica Ray Walls (14)
Queen Anne High School, Broomhead Parks

Layers Of Pain

When you say it, it's funny,
But is it really?
Words like knives,
Hate dipped in honey.

Strangers in my head,
They think they can own me,
Throw my dreams in the bin,
All the hurt beneath my skin.

I don't recall the girl in the mirror,
Keeping all the feelings
Bottled up,
Until the dam breaks...

Lucy Harrison (12)
Queen Anne High School, Broomhead Parks

The Grumpy Cat Diaries

Dear Diary,
Day no. 126 of torture.

Today, my pet human gave me no food,
No matter how much I let out
Blood-curdling whines
And ear-splitting screeches.
I hate humans.
That ignorant parasite
Spent most of his day
Staring at a glowing box,
But, when I tried to see what was stealing
His somewhat limited attention,
He pushed me off the table!
How dare he!

Dear Diary,
Day no. 127 of torture.

I ran off to visit my pal, Henry,
And we terrorised his human together,
It was elating!
When I got back, the sun was setting
And my human was wimping about,
As per usual when I go out,
Pathetic.
I leapt through the window and
As soon as his beady, little black eyes saw me,

He immediately rushed over
And spread his arms out wide,
Uh oh!
I acted quick and hissed to keep him away,
It didn't work.
I was swiftly embraced in a 'hug'.
I hate humans.

Harry Clark (12)
Ratcliffe College, Ratcliffe On The Wreake

Dysphoric

Her mind breaks,
Her headache turns into heartache,
Her hands shake
With the crushing feeling of being a disgrace.

Up early in the morning,
Up late at night,
The strictures of her wardens
In her head, these words taken flight.

Authoritarian adults
Produce demeaning words,
She thought she'd grown numb to them
But each word strikes a chord

And she's drowning in the stress
Of meeting expectations
And she's choking on the mess
She's decided is her life.

Because, she knows, or she thinks,
That it's best for her to strive
To isolate herself
And impress overbearing forebears.

But, now and then, she wonders
Where, oh, where,
Is her happiness and love,
Creativity and joy?

She's buried her identity,
Now, she's but an empty entity.

Arifah Suleiman (15)
Ratcliffe College, Ratcliffe On The Wreake

Boris Johnson

Today, I slammed the door
At number 10 Downing Street,
My thick blonde hair brushed
My googly, blue eyes,
As Larry, the cat, was scratching away
At the lovely, new carpet,
Bang! Bang! Bang!

A large fist smacked
The outside of my bedroom door,
"Boris! What have you done, ya imbecile!"
Said Theresa May,
My heart stopped in confusion.

Opening my Top Secret notepad,
Which I stole from my English teacher,
Miss Battle-Axe,
Putting my pencil to paper
I thought Jeremy Hunt could've done
A better job than I had.

Thomas Urwin (12)
Ratcliffe College, Ratcliffe On The Wreake

On The Edge

Watching and waiting,
My mind in knots,
Adrenaline in my heart,
Continuously beating.

Messing with my mind,
Cowering every time I hear a sound,
Thinking endlessly
About my life so far.

Stuck, waiting for freedom
To escape the darkness,
A chance to be free,
If only for a second, but that is just reality.

Lonely and lost,
Not anyone on my side,
My fate awaits,
Along with my...
Execution!

Spike Chapman (11)
Ratcliffe College, Ratcliffe On The Wreake

Childhood In Iraq

Rubble lies behind me
Fear swiftly reignites in my heart
My livelihood blown to pieces
I can't handle the pressure that war has dropped upon me
It turned days and nights into the nightmare of my life
My brother running away to commit himself to a hopeless cause
Dying in days.

My schools, my neighbourhood, blown away like dust
In seconds
My mother holds me tight and I hold her
"It's time to leave," she speaks calmly
I know it's time to flee.

Matthew Anderson
Shawlands Academy, Glasgow

Fernando Rickson

To go from sprinting around a football field
To being unable to move.

To go from being able to speak my feelings
To being completely mute.

To go from a Rangers and Dutch hero
Straight to a legend.

The struggle was real
But now I can feel
For I am free once more
In pain no more.

Motor Neurone may have won
But now I'm able to have some fun
Goodbye world, goodbye Rangers
Fernando Ricksen is number one.

Nikolas Thornton Miller (13)
Shawlands Academy, Glasgow

MLK Jr

Segregated through life
Born black
Lived black
Killed black.

Racism at its peak
Discrimination was a feat
Rules set in
The air of jail
Was a common affair.

Different buses, different lives
No luxuries 'cause I wasn't white
Stood up, protested
Gave speeches, attended meetings.

Gave voice to my dream
Became immortalised
Martin Luther
King Junior.

Born black
Died black
Killed...
For being black.

Swaraj Virdi
Shawlands Academy, Glasgow

The Crash

When I got there I was sitting in the cockpit thundering down the runway...
I'm in the air doing a loop. No! No! I'm too low, need to eject.

When I got there I was among hundreds, the plane was looping.
Oh no! The pilot can't pull out. No! There's an explosion, red and black, the plane's gone.

When I got there I was in a car, this plane was thundering down, no!
I don't crash. *Boom!* Red and black... I'm now in hospital... I'm alive!

When I got there, there were fires, smashed cars, debris and bodies,
ambulances, injured people on stretchers being loaded inside the ambulances.

When I got there the bodies were in bags, there was nothing more than wreaths of flowers with photos of victims, crying family members and untouched debris and what was left of the Hawker Hunter.

Matthew Timothy Levitt (11)
Slindon College, Arundel

Life As A Pumpkin

In the early hours of the morning, I was woken up with a
loud noise
A large blue box was coming towards me
As it was coming towards me I yelled,
"What the hell?"

A massive blade chopped my root, my lifeline!
I stopped growing,
"Where am I going?"
I was chucked into a massive lorry
Lots of other pumpkins around me.

I awoke in a cardboard box
A horrible, little kid, munching on sweets
Grabbed me with his sticky hands!
"Put me down,
You little clown!"

That chubby kid
Cut off my head
Scooped out my insides
And ate them!

He cut eyes out in my skin
And gave me a creepy smile
And then came a bright orange light
Just as I thought it was alright
I felt the burning, burning, burning!

I'm a pumpkin
Get me out of here!

Reece Anderson (14)
Slindon College, Arundel

Being A Teen

I watched in the playground as the bully walked away
The grade 4 boy was lying on the ground in pain
I headed over towards him and saw him bruised in the hay
Then he talked me through his pain.

The bully, a grade 9, bullying a grade 4
Why did he pick this boy and what pleasure does he get
when they cry?
Bullying, and what for?
For the pleasure they get when he makes them cry.

The kid comes over in tears, talks to me, "It's too much," he
says
The bully walks past us and spits our way.

The kid goes home that night and doesn't come in the next
day, the next week
He's gone now, gone for good, he died for nothing
Why does this bully pick upon the weak?
When all he got was nothing
But a few laughs.
Stop bullying now.

Olly Skinner (15)
Slindon College, Arundel

Reggie's Weekend

My world is weird because I only see legs and feet.
I wish that I could sit up at the table with the big people
But no, I'm stuck down here eating
And drinking out of a dirty bowl.
And the most annoying thing is when I call them,
They just ignore me.
But when they call me, I listen like a good little boy
And I go to them.
I don't know why but when I jump onto the table,
For fish and chips, they get angry for some reason.
All I wanted was chips.
But when I get lucky, which is very rare,
I might get one or two chips.
And for some odd reason, when I need the toilet
They just put me in the rain like I did something wrong.
And apparently they take me on walks
When actually I drag them wherever we go.

Leyton Partridge (11)
Slindon College, Arundel

Victor Ludorum

Boredom Dulorem
The Victor Ludorum
That's when I found out I canny afford 'em
Thanks for attention, fame, good fortune.

Mind: Win the race
Keep a straight face
These shortie slow wannabes could never
Focus, god sake
And win the race
You're 6ft 2, skinny, built like Usain
They've been much less ya'll.

One thousand eight hundred metres in total
Chasin' that cheque, win that -
Swiping that Visa.

Twenty-nineteen is the worst year ever
Dunno how I managed to pull through
Adults talk down (skinny)
Stay and be -

Strong, deservin'
Bad (I'm sorry)
Depends on mood
Thrive above
Show no care

For those who dare
Show 'em you don't care.

Tom Crane (14)
Slindon College, Arundel

Poet's Block

I'm trying to make an original poem but I'm struggling on doing it.
I've been given many ideas but none of them seems fun enough.
I thought of doing a weird one but that's for the stories I do, not poems.
I thought of doing one on world leaders but that would be too controversial.
I thought of doing one on everyone in the classroom but people would bully me.
I thought of doing one on computers but I'm not in Year 7.
I thought of doing one on people I don't like but they would bully me for that.
They started bullying me anyway
So I called the military and got them eliminated.
Now I can do whatever I want
And I don't have to write any poems.

Theo Stapleton (15)
Slindon College, Arundel

Trump Life

My name is Donald Trump
I am the greatest of them all
I have the greatest haircut of them all
My idea of the Mexican wall was the greatest idea of them
all
I think I should not be impeached because I am the greatest
man of them all
My TV show, The Apprentice' was my idea not the British
Because it was the greatest TV show of them all
I'm not a racist because I am the greatest
I'm not stupid because I am the greatest
My best friend is Boris Johnson because we are the greatest
of them all
I hate Kim Jong-un because he is not the greatest
The reason I do these things is because I am the greatest in
the world.

Cormac Wilson (15)

Slindon College, Arundel

Differences

Just because we look the same
doesn't mean we are the same.

So when the teacher calls my name
either one of us can take the blame.

But my brother likes sport
and I just like to go for long walks.

My brother likes to chatter
but I don't think anything he says will even matter.

And even though I'm different on the outside
he's still my identical twin.

Charlie Wreford (11)
Slindon College, Arundel

I Am Billy Kimber

I am Billy Kimber, king of the races,
If you don't obey my orders
I will have you shot up against a post.
Some people rebel against me.
I am the law.
This is my world.
The world leaders have to bow down to me or die.
I do not care about the poor,
Nobody stands a chance against me.
I have gone through torture before
I still feel the pain that was before I owned the races.

Samuel Ghebre Ghiorgios (11)

Slindon College, Arundel

Sam Pilgrim

I'm at the start gate,
Blood is pumping through my veins,
It feels like the bike is part of me,
I am ready to go.

I'm going super fast,
The wind is rushing past me,
The bumps are rattling my bones,
The trees are whizzing past.

The crowd goes wild
As I go through the finish line,
Cheering and clapping,
I end with a skid,
The rush has gone.

Archie Weller (14)
Slindon College, Arundel

Marmite

As I sit on the table being ignored
I think, *why do people despise me?*
However, some people are flawed
And even idolise me.

"It's the worst form of yeast!"
Cries one side of the table.
"Shut up you beast,
It's delicious on a bagel!"

It's all a matter of taste
I'm just a yeast-based paste.

Leo Mitchener (15)
Slindon College, Arundel

The Trenches

(Dedicated to John Miles, a soldier from Slindon who died during WWI)

As I walked down the trench it was horrible.
There was a stench,
It was loud, it was muddy and cramped.
I heard a whistle of a shell then *boom!*
It exploded right behind me.
I had whiplash after it.
Then the major shouted, "To the ladders, men."
Then he blew the whistle,
I ran towards the black icy abyss...

Lenny Hopkins (11)
Slindon College, Arundel

We Love The Earth

We love the Earth, that's what people say,
But looking down from here, I don't see it that way,
You shoot your people,
You destroy my trees,
You pollute the air and suffocate the seas,
My creatures are dying, can you not see?
Screaming out in pain, I want them to be free,

We love the Earth, that's what they always say,
I see no difference since the last protest you made,
You say #savetheturtles, yet you take it for a joke,
But, if you cared to notice they could go down in smoke,
I should have known since you bit that poison apple,
That taking you along was going to be a gamble,

We love the Earth, they say again,
I really don't know how to describe my pain,
I have been thinking and now I know,
The only way to save this planet is to destroy it whole,
Goodbye my animals, I will see you soon,
Goodbye my fish, just for today,
I promise to make your descendants better, okay.
Goodbye humans that I will not miss,
I will be talking to the Lord about your 'bliss'.

Joseph Semourson (13)
St Augustine's RC School, Scarborough

The Wretched Daughter

Suffocated. Empty. Misplaced. Lost. Fractured.
Broken.
Akin a living platter of pity.

A replica of a marionette,
Contrived to comply.
A counterfeit smile, a clandestine lie
An eternal supernova.

Blockade the door.
Seal the curtains.
Breathe.
Deeply grieving and mourning.
The heartening solace of the darkness.

She touches her heart, her soul-
Aches. Yet -
She does not dare,
Unravel elsewhere.

Bury and suppress.
Over-casted emotions,
Masks upon masks,
Charades upon charades,
Facades upon facades.

Acts deceitfully portrayed.
Like an actress,
Mastered her craft.

Caught in a web
Or a trap?
Longing for council
Anything for her troubled self.

A game she plays
Of fatal flaws.
She tries and tries
Only, for the rain of disappointment
To befall her -
Completely.

Silence. Only the clouds raging conflict.
She bore into one's eyes.
Resentment, disbelief, incredulity
But most importantly,
The gauging heaviness of her heart.

Introductions of diversions
Vanquished the daughter's dollar from one's eyes.
Blissful innocent ignorant.
Discourse enters, the war had not yet concluded.

Tick-tock the darkness takes control -
A black entity pulling her deeper
Till she is no more.

Traumas roll, exhausting.
Writings of surplus sorrow.
Tear-stained,

Blurred.
Crimson flickers,
"Goodbye."

Angela Valsan (14)
St Augustine's RC School, Scarborough

An Interpretation Of Death

Everyone has a time,
I fashion them like a clock for their pretty chime,
I like to take them in my palm,
Bring them close to hear its charm,

I'm feared and hated,
But worshipped and feted,
Always watching over your time
And, eventually turning off your clock's rhyme,

Many people have created my form,
Whether dark, brooding or fury storm,
You seem to despise my hard eyes,
But never truly understand why,

You lose and you've lost,
But don't make that cost,
Your happiness is notably at my dispense,
But that's only in the present tense,

Your clock, your life,
I can cut them with a butter knife,
But nature is fair and just
And I don't want your clock to rust,

As I take them from their chains,
The tears below begin to rain,
It's okay to grieve and lose,
This is only my point of view.

Iona Grassam
St Augustine's RC School, Scarborough

When Will It Change?

When will it change?
The hurt, the pain,
The constant remarks,
That you think makes you smart,
The whispering in the halls,
The frequent 'secret calls',
The comments shouted in the middle of class,
That cut deeper than a shard of glass,
This hurt gets worse each day,
You have no idea of my dismay,
I don't want to blame just you,
But I just don't know what to do,
I cry on the way home,
But you would never know,
Because I will never show,
My hands shake when I see you
But you will never have a clue,
The smile is just a cover-up,
And so is all this makeup,
I sit alone,
Blocked you from my phone,
I am always judged
And in the halls, I'm shoved,
Everyone's life is hard,
It's just the luck of the card,

Life's one big game,
Someone must take the blame,
Me.

Katie Robinson (13)
St Augustine's RC School, Scarborough

Outsider

I had a love but then we broke,
I was abused but never spoke.
Started fighting because of the anger,
Drinking and smoking made me an outsider.
My grandma got cancer,
I remember the day I called her but no answer.
I was betrayed by the world,
Where were my mother and father?
No sister, no brother, alone that's what I was,
It was together forever then I hit pause.
Didn't know how to act when I got pregnant because...
My life was a hot mess,
No room on a street for another child that was.

Emily Penfold (13)
St Augustine's RC School, Scarborough

Internet Girls

Internet girls,
who we aspire to be.
Internet girls,
nothing like you and me.
Internet girls,
with marks on your wrists.
Internet girls,
are you happy with this?
We cut off our toes just to make a shoe fit,
Internet girls,
are you happy about this?
We starve ourselves and make up our lives
just to fit in with your humankind...

Hannah Lilian Grace Curtis (13)
St Augustine's RC School, Scarborough

At The Fair

I look up and down
When I'm in town
Up so high
I could touch the sky
On a roller coaster
As I get closer and closer
I scream
I wake up
It was all a dream.

Jessica May Duckering (12)
St Augustine's RC School, Scarborough

From The Fountain Pen Of President Bolsonaro

Suddenly, I feel a tight, squeezing pain
And I am lurched, helplessly, into the vast, open-air,
Then, after seeing a familiar shape resting on the table,
I feel lightheaded and completely vulnerable.
Below me, I see a form, a contract,
In my pain, weirdly, I focus on the words below,
I make out sixteen-million dollars
For out-of-control wildfires,
The loss of animals and life,
The growth of agricultural land,
The death of indigenous tribes,
A stop to all this terror,
Then...
A blank space.
I then feel my head brushing against the paper
And
Where the blank space had just been, an answer:
No.
Suddenly, my pain returned,
Not the tight, squeezing pain from before,
No, a great pain from within,
A pain of sadness,
A pain of sorrow,
A pain of loss of what I've just done...

Dylan Willer-Watson (12)

St Christopher Senior School, Letchworth Garden City

Never-Ending Pain

(A poem from the perspective of a cat's hair)

Constant pain, no, *stop!*
To this madness!
No rest!
No sleep!
No care!
Every day, the death of my brethren,
A rough tongue pulling me away,
Destroyed under tons of fat,
Rubbed against
Jagged stones,
Scratchy objects,
Worst of all -
The thought that this will not change.
Why? Why? Why?

Jack Boo Milton-Herron (12)

St Christopher Senior School, Letchworth Garden City

In My Hands

Not every light is bright,
Not every tree is tall,
Feel the darkness from the night,
Accept it or you'll fall.

Something broken can be fixed,
Something better can be made,
When two things are often mixed,
The third one might just fade.

One might have the power
But the other has the faith,
It ticks every hour,
You don't want to be late.

Keep everything aside,
End it once and for all,
You were born to fight the tide,
Rest after you break the wall.

Stay focused on your goal,
That's what helps you on your way,
Everybody has a soul,
Don't let someone steal your day.

Keyuri Sachin Ade (14)
St Leonards School, The Pends

The Truth About The World Today

The truth about the world we live in today,
Is so shocking, we push the accurate negativity away,
We don't concentrate on the problems we have,
Instead, we install the latest app.

We live in a world where we don't show love,
Children as young as sixteen running around with guns,
We tell 'white lies' in order to protect ourselves,
They'll eventually take another life.

When we look at the world, it is sugar-coated,
Children die never knowing the feeling of being bloated,
We see adverts showing the poor,
We're lucky our beds aren't the mud floor.

The new generation doesn't see the reality,
It's like there's wool pulled over their eyes,
In society, it seems normal to take others' lives.

Through their eyes, they must not see,
That the effects of their actions are ridiculously deep,
They show no sorrow,
Say no prayers,
They're young and blinded,
Unfortunately.

Millie-Leigh Ashby (15)
St Thomas Centre Upper School, Blackburn

Nothing Lasts Forever

I have objects stacked against me,
Objects pinned through my being,
For my protection, they paid the fee,
Little do they know what I am seeing.

I have witnessed all the emotions,
Laughter, pain, rage and more,
People received major promotions,
For working until their heads were sore.

My master chose me to serve his purpose,
His eyes were beaming with glee,
His wife didn't want me to be a circus,
I would have jumped when they got the key.

Now, the master has long since gone free,
His wife slowly catching up,
But their family lives within me,
Their children, grandchildren and pup.

I look at everything that they do,
I listen to everything that they say,
If I'm ever broken by somebody new,
I'll remember this family every day.

Aiden Joseph Jagdeo (13)
Thames Christian School, Clapham

Missing

You daily see posters
Of people you
Don't know,
With the label, entitled,
Missing.
It's help that you want to show
But you only see the side effect,
Not the family.
You see the number,
But you don't dial,
Not even a trial
Because, eventually, you'll feel your heart sinking,
Like a baby down the River Nile,
You'd rather keep it real
And keep your mouth sealed,
Than take the real deal.

Then, karma reacts,
It starts with death
And the family never comes back.
With the devil knocking on your door,
Waiting to stuff your life in a sack,
A sack you can't open,
And the positive you'll lack.

You may not let it happen,
But it has other plans,

Temptation seems to be holding your hand,
Yet, it's pushing you down
With no reason to stand
And you have a decision to run away since
You think you're separate from God's plan,
So you land on a highway
Away from your homeland.

Yet, you still don't realise what *Missing* is,
Because *Missing* is a state that's been eternal for years
And soulmates and friends that are filled with tears
Miss their friend who left his careers
And the episode,
Your episode,
Your season,
Has been cut down with devilish shears.

So, now, you're truly *Missing*,
You feel no way of living,
Yet, *Missing*, is no feeling,
It's a thing,
You've missed your heavenly bus,
It's moving,
You can't go back because
The prodigal son's part is finished,
You've missed your life,
Your goal,
Your family,

Your home
And you, when you think it couldn't end too soon
There'll be demons round you repeating,
"Rest in peace," in your tomb.

Isaiah Boyd (13)
Thames Christian School, Clapham

Achieving Sports Goals

I wake up every morning,
I want to play ball,
After I stop yawning,
I need to play ball.

I always aim high,
I cannot lie,
I always work hard,
It's from the heart.

Sport is my dream,
I always go extreme,
I run like a beam,
I work in my team.

I want to achieve my goals
Each and every day,
I sometimes run around poles,
Then I shout, "Hooray!"

I practice all the time,
I will never stop,
Let's make this poem rhyme
Because it's sport o'clock.

I have a positive mindset,
So, I don't give up,
I say I can't do it yet,
That makes me who I am today!

Campbell Robert Bright (11)
Thames Christian School, Clapham

I Do Have Feelings

I stand here, all day and night,
So innocent and motionless,
My peace, however, is never quite
Respected how I would like.

People walk past me throughout the day,
As I curiously watch what's going on,
I like to rest but I have to say
Some people do disrespect me.

My roots they do kick
As they walk all around me
And my leaves they do pick
As they hurry on past me.

Children come and climb up me,
Pulling firmly on my branches,
The pain in me, they do not see,
Yet I still worry for their safety.

Apart from that, my life's alright,
It's never boring, never hectic,
With a nice, calm night
And a peaceful day.

But, just as I thought my life was okay,
The lumberjacks come to inspect me,
Oh, that was a very dreaded day
When they searched me for imperfections.

"This tree looks ever so good,
It's wonderfully perfect in every way,
Imagine what we can do with the wood,
I think this is the one to cut down!"

They returned the next week,
Armed with lots of equipment,
If only I could shout, or even speak,
I'd say, "Leave me alone, I'm happy like this!"

Worry then started to fiercely attack me
As they prepared all the violent machines,
How could I say I'm a normal tree,
So they'd go away and let me be.

I suppose I'll just have to suffer the pain,
Of the blades that will cut me so sharply,
I think the people are rather insane
To murder me without any shame.

As one last word, I'd like to say,
Imagine if someone cut you down,
How would you feel that very day
Without a choice but to suffer?

Cecilia Hayward-Bhikha (13)
Thames Christian School, Clapham

Through Asia's Eyes

Hi, I'm Asia,
I'm a dog,
It's funny because humans always get what they want,
For example, they go on the couch, or eat food in front of me,
Sometimes I'm confused about this, but I guess this is just how life goes.

I love tennis balls, rocks and sticks
But that's not all I love,
Food and running around,
My favourite is family!
And that's what family is,
Different people's differences together.

Jael Schmidt (11)
Thames Christian School, Clapham

Death Row

Nowhere to run, nowhere to go,
Now that I'm stuck on a death row,
Woe is me,
Happiness is a thing I can't conceive,
I begged and pleaded
But my compassion was not received,
My suffering, they didn't believe,
I'm losing my sanity,
"End me now!" I cried in agony,
Loneliness is eating me up like a broken tree,
What's hurting me is that I know it won't end happily,
The days pass by, taunting me,
I wish I could rewind time, I feel so guilty.

Hamzah Gaffar (11)
The City Of Leicester College, Evington

Death Row

Death row, death row, my turn is to go to heaven,
There is nothing to prevent this conundrum,
My friends and me and people from my family tree,
We are so hungry.

So much controversy,
Scarce amount of amnesty,
Rumble, rumble, rumble,
Tumble, tumble, tumble.

The clouds are raging,
We are ageing,
Pow!
Wow!

We are free,
My parents found me!

Teghvir Singh (11)
The City Of Leicester College, Evington

Woman Football Player

Butterflies erupting from the stomach up,
Cold upthrust of confidence,
Whistle blown, head up,
The ball rolling towards you,
Motionless,
Hearts thumping to the beat of the ball,
It's within your grasp, nervously but confident,
Dribbling towards the opening goal,
Thinking it's just you and the goal, just you and the goal,
Motionless,
Roar of crowds raising,
Complete silence
As the ball stumbles into the goal,
The keeper leaping forward,
You wondering if it's in,
Motionless,
The sudden, daunting thought of this being your last
chance,
It hits the back of the net, swaying it side-to-side,
Sound floods back in,
Cheers of celebration,
Echoes in the background,
Making your team proud,
Motionless.

Lexxie Blythe
The FitzWimarc School, Rayleigh

Lost

Have you felt
Unheard, neglected, threatened?
Like you're in a dark room with no door.
No escape.
No articulation.

What if the world crumbled down and you were left alone.
What if you were stranded with nowhere to go.
Arrived but never returned.

Trudging on and on with no sense of direction
In severe need of nurturance.
No succour.
No euphoria.

What if a pack of hungry lions cornered you with no way out.
What if your tears just dropped into a cavernous, leaden ocean.
With no thought or care.

That is the feeling of hollow unfamiliarity.
That is the feeling of being estranged, alienated...
That is the feeling of being *lost*.

Aneesha Chakraborty (11)
The Lady Eleanor Holles School, Hampton

The Last Day

It was a dark, cold, misty morning and it was silent,
As if an animal kingdom had become extinct.
I was crying and crying, longing for help,
It was my final day, my final day on this planet,
I was trembling and shaking everywhere.

The blinding light leapt into my direction of sight,
It was like a leopard cantering and leaping straight into me.
I moved my head suddenly to the opposite direction,
So I did not have to encounter the blinding light.

I suddenly heard staggering footsteps coming towards my direction,
From that moment I knew it was it, I felt horrified.
I just did not believe it was the end of my life,
I looked vividly to one side of the prison,
And saw a dark enclosed shadow approaching my cell.

The figure stopped and glared into my direction as I gave a sudden shudder,
The figure unlocked my cell with a large thick metal key.
I dragged myself to stand up and tread to the figure's direction,
The figure held an object in his hand,
The object gave a deafening firing sound and I fell to the floor with a loud thud.

Max Briffett (14)
The Oratory School, Woodcote

One Boy, Two Minds

He knows that feeling,
It's something you can't control,
It's a feeling unfelt before,
Where you're trying to find your soul.

He knows it's a harsh feeling,
But he thought he was tough,
He thinks he can control it,
But enough is enough.

Enough of the loneliness,
Enough of the pain,
Enough of the emptiness
Because there is no gain.

He started at two,
He lost a lot,
His friends, his family,
Himself too.

His dad moved away,
Started a new life,
Without him or his mum,
As well as a new wife.

He often found himself thinking,
Do they know what it's like?
To feel their confidence shrinking,
To cry and be ashamed of it.

To feel that empty,
To think no one cares,
To wish someone would ask,
"How are you?"

People would say go to your parents,
But he only had one,
He had to get away from his problem,
It all seemed a real task.

Why couldn't he though? he asked himself,
There was no way round it,
But people started to notice,
So he had to hide the embarrassment of his mental state.

Now he is eleven,
Finished primary,
But he still felt so alone,
He was wary of that.

He had got through six years of bullying,
Bullied about his constant long face, facial expressions and
weight,
How bad could secondary be?
He was in constant fear, a state.

Through those years he put on this other mind,
This alter ego,
This happy and laughing pretend little boy,

So no one could know how he cried every night
And wished he wasn't here.

But he caught a hold of something,
A lifeline,
This new school had offered him,
For once he felt loved and cared for.

He took this and now is in a stable state,
It was something he had never felt before,
He has bad days,
Where family, school and people put him down.

But he has learnt to regain that strength,
That willingness to care about his life,
Knowing he meant something to that person or people,
That the meanies meant nothing.

He knew his life did matter,
That he shouldn't take it, it would cause too much pain,
Just like everyone else,
He mattered.

He knows he did things he regretted,
Some are imprinted in his life forever,
But he didn't let them get him down anymore,
He knew there were people to help anywhere and whenever.

Depression is real,
It's not 'a grab for attention',

It happens to real people with real feelings,
Who knows it could be happening to someone so close to
you?

Depression is a real thing,
It's a bad mental state,
It's something that likes to cling
He kept silent and for that he paid.

Now he encourages you,
To come forward,
He encourages you to get help,
Because he knows there are people who care.

He says you don't have to do this alone,
You don't have to do things to yourself to try and make
yourself feel better,
He knows it doesn't work,
He goes by one simple phrase.

Don't live your life in the shadows,
Don't be ashamed to say how you feel
And come forward.

Oliver Mark Francis Davies Byron (15)
The Oratory School, Woodcote

Death Row

I woke up staring at the vivid white ceiling,
I stepped over to my sink and I looked up to the cracked mirror
To see my face trembling with fear
Of the lethal injection
But I stayed strong.
I looked around the small, plain white room of isolation
And could only hope at this point,
I didn't know why but it just felt right.

My last meal
I didn't know what to choose for my last meal
It hadn't quite crossed my mind
When death was so near
So I settled on some Rice Krispies,
I glanced down at the bowl of cereal
Thinking of the man that got stopped.

It was time, all strapped to the bed,
Vulnerable like a lost baby in a crowd,
My time had come,
Rapidly scanning everything in the room as a last vision,
Scanning every crevice clearly.

I had been injected,
All sixteen years leading up to this moment
I didn't bother restraining
I tried to think of memories that I had when I was a kid

But all I could think about was when the judge called me guilty
And now here I was, getting executed.

After all, I was guilty.

Lawrence Ward (13)
The Oratory School, Woodcote

Winston Churchill

It is a dark, misty evening,
The wind howling through the trees,
The snow is peacefully landing,
As white as a blanket.
I am feeling rather nervous
As I am about to give a speech.

Why should we let him conquer?
Why should we allow him to get away with killing people?
Why should we allow him to turn us inside out?
We will fight against him and we will win!

France might have been taken,
We might be in a full-fledged retreat,
Like mice running away from cats,
But why don't we be that one mouse that fights back,
That one little boy that stands up to the bully?
Don't give up
When we still have the power to fight back.

We will make mistakes
But we can fix them.
A mistake can cause an injury
But the comeback can save a country
And we will come back
We will get France back
And we will end this war!

My mind is running away with me
But I am desperate to win,
Sweat trickling down my face
And my heart hammering like a drum
But this is for one reason:
My country is relying on me.

Milo Briffett (13)
The Oratory School, Woodcote

Death Row

I'm all alone in this cold, dark and disgusting room,
Nobody to talk to, the deafening noise of the rats in the
walls,
The boredom is killing me as I speak,
As the noise stopped, everything went out.

As I long for days to pass, I sit there looking back at the
past,
From this beast that awaits to kill me and eat my sanity
And spit away my soul to hell,
I looked back on the past,
I remembered those days where the rain used to fall
Hard on the ground,
But also the shiny and hot days.

And still as the evening ends the moon
And the stars fill the night sky lighting it bright
As the breeze blows and the tide flows,
But this is all a dream,
The death is coming right around the corner,
As I lay there, I thought, *would it ever guide me the right
way?*

Toby Martin (14)
The Oratory School, Woodcote

A Day Of A Fireman

6am sharp, the alarm clock sounds,
My sleep pattern shattered and perplexed,
The morning is tranquil though in my mind,
I sense a storm brewing and bubbling,
And the air thick and foreboding.

I suit myself with the dense attire,
The stench repulsive from yesterday.
My heavy legs shove me out the door and into the truck,
As I await today's challenges.

The radio calls, the sirens on, I charge towards the scene,
I enter the smoky abyss,
Hearing a bellow shutter down the hall,
I perform the daring routine,
Entering the mouth of the dragon
And winning!

With the person rescued and the flames kept subtle I head back,
Although my break is short and abrupt,
As the radio calls again,
Time to be the humble hero,
No time for celebrations.

Gabriel Whelpton (14)
The Oratory School, Woodcote

Death Row

The corridor that connected all the rooms fell silent,
The rain outside could be heard echoing on the windows,
My mind couldn't drift off knowing that it could be my turn,
As soon as I got in here, losing track of time sent me crazy.

Once a week a guard came round to ask my preferred meal,
The guard would be the only external being we'd see,
As inmates gave their meals, the guard would laugh,
knowing we'd never get it,
Some people made it a game picking the meal they wanted,
knowing they would never get it.

When the guard came in to collect people's meals, someone
would always go,
The inmates would sometimes bet on who would be taken
out next,
People that were there at the beginning stayed there,
The new ones always went first.

Jonny Wainhouse (13)
The Oratory School, Woodcote

Leicester City's Comeback Poem 2015/2016

The odds were 5000/1
Our chances of winning the league were gone
With a new manager on hand
Our aim was to win the grand slam.

With Vardy, Mahrez and Amartey
If we won the fans would have a party
Fans were imagining us winning the cup
Until we had Liverpool first game up!

This game ended with a draw at Anfield
Our defence was nothing like a shield
By Christmas we were thirty-five points up
Santa must have given us good luck.

We won, we lost, we drew
Luckily none of the players got the flu
Against all odds, we battled through
To lift the cup to the sea of blue!

Henry Watson (14)
The Oratory School, Woodcote

No One Wins In War

Inspired by my great-grandad.

No one wins in war,
There is no need for it anymore,
I battled and fought,
Almost lost my life,
Leaving behind a beautiful wife,
With the children I had taught,
To talk and to walk.

Killing men I had never seen,
Who might have been friends,
If we had met on another day.
It was the worst I've ever been,
But instead of war,
There must be another way.

Fighting is always wrong,
No matter what it says in the song,
We must always get along.
Life is a gift,
We must value everyone,
We are all different,
But we all breathe the same.

George Henry Clark (13)
The Oratory School, Woodcote

Spider-Man

"Spider-Man," they call,
I swing, I zing and I swoop in for the criminals,
Raging away in their cars,
Driving carelessly away.

I race to the scene,
Crowds gathering,
All panicking.

I can spin a spider net,
A net no other human could.
I swoop, fly and twist,
Capturing those I miss.

I'm a hero, the one they see,
Always calling on my mighty strength,
My legs are as strong as two men's combined,
My webs would break a man's skull in two,
Webs of steel, webs of might.

Callum Griffith (13)
The Oratory School, Woodcote

The Story Of A Broken Soul

In a chamber of a dead dream,
Where living seems extreme,
Through the dark I crawl,
To a land that missed us all,
For a crime I did not commit,
And it breaks my heart a bit.

Next day my life will end,
But my mind shall not bend,
Even though my heart cannot still mend,
When I go away,
My soul will fly away,
And up there it will stay.

I wish my family had not grieved,
So I will be relieved,
And my truth shall be believed.

George Maniadakis (14)
The Oratory School, Woodcote

Son Of An Immigrant

The son of the immigrant,
This is what I am,
They gave up so much for me,
And now I have to do the same for them.

Helping them with bills,
Because they helped me get the skill.
They moved here for my life,
So I move my life for them.

Now I have mental health issues,
But they have already done too much,
So I will hide this last thing,
So they can be at peace for the peace they gave me.

Jake Ford (14)
The Oratory School, Woodcote

Before It's Too Late

Like a rat in a cage, I am treated like vermin,
The noose's hands around my neck, my crime I couldn't
determine.
Blindfolded; I am visionless to the people but not deaf to
their noises,
Squawking, "Queer, gay, waste of space," with raucous,
ruthless voices.

I am brittle to these words - just a simple man in love,
We fit together perfectly, just like a hand in glove.
He gives me happiness, purpose, and a reason to climb,
Since when was sharing your life with someone such an
unspeakable crime?

My clothes are torn, for I am just an animal,
My rights are irrelevant, like those of a cannibal.
I am told to step forward, aware of my fate,
I attempt to scream my lover's name, before it's too late.

Face sweating, palms clammy, yet I am bitterly cold,
Why must our sexualities conceal our hearts of gold?
I am weak and insignificant, confined by vicious beasts,
I'm just a filthy, vulgar rodent, soon to be deceased.

Chanting falcons growing louder; shrieking their vile song,
I pray that in the future, who you love stops being wrong.
They're tightening the rope, and I cry at what's to come,
The floor dissolves beneath my feet and, with that, I
succumb.

Hannah Cain
The Stanway School, Stanway

Mental Health

Mental illness sucks,
They always tell to 'just look up'.
To the people that were just like me,
When they were in secondary,
They don't understand that
Some days, you're down,
Some days, you're fine,
Then, some days, you're feeling absolutely divine.

Sometimes, it's the little things that hold me down,
Like people saying, "Why that frown?"
But, if you know what I've been through,
You'll want to scream what you've been through too.

Cry, shout and pace about,
Trying to let all your anxiety out.
You try to break free but you just know
It will never ever let you go.

Being a teen is hard to describe,
You pretend you're great but you're living a lie.

Although all that I've said is true,
There is one last thing I need to tell you.
Even though most days are blue,
You just have to believe in you
And, as the saying goes,
Every cloud has a silver lining.

Oriana Barnard (12)
The Stanway School, Stanway

Mirror, Mirror

The joy of wearing the rosy dress soon faded from her face
And was replaced with displeasure at each outfit that her
wardrobe had to offer,
It was always the same in the end.

Life as a mirror...
How can I explain?
Well...
Pleasure comes and goes,
It's almost as if my life is a lie,
Not just a white lie,
I suppose it gets irritating,
Me, always copying the one looking in on me,
But I have a secret.

It's a secret from everyone,
Even her,
I've known Ashley her whole life
From her first steps,
To the daily struggle to get out of her bed this morning,
I've stood dormant in the corner of her room these last
fifteen years.

My duty is to mimic,
To copy,
But ever since the day, Ashley...
Well...
I've been lying,

Making Ashley pleased once again,
I'd keep going,
But someone found out...

Martha Elliot (13)
The Stanway School, Stanway

Flaming Arrow

Flicker, flicker,
Hiss, spit,
Burning through the night,
Brighter, brighter,
Smoulder, glow,
Raging through the dark.

Whistle, whistle,
Shriek, buzz,
Flying through the night,
Glide, glide,
Spin, curve,
Whizzing through the dark.

Samuel Thompson (12)
The Stanway School, Stanway

Kylie Jenner

Big lights flashing,
Bank accounts cashing,
Fancy clothes and all

That's the life they show on cameras
That's not the life at all:
Hate comments
The lip fillers were meant
But I have a story, don't you know
I'm insecure
"Are you really sure?"
They ask.
They don't know the nights I've spent weeping with my phone,
They don't know how I hate myself to the bone.
"Plastic! All fake!" they shout.
I'm real! I'm real! I post with a pout
They don't know the days I spend working out
And all they do is sit on the couch and flout.

You see, I never asked for this,
This fame, this life.
But that's how the world works. I guess.
While I go to the gym to stay fit
You'll be out buying that Kylie Jenner lip kit.

Sivanky Uthayakumar (14)
The Tiffin Girls' School, Kingston Upon Thames

Helping Boris

My name is Nathaniel,
You might not know me,
But you have seen me
On your flatscreen TV.
So, who am I?
I'm not a person,
But I help them.
I help others identify a human,
I help barbers get paid,
Yes, I'm your hair.
So, which human do I help?
That's the problem,
His name is Boris.

I'm with him when he goes on stage
And on those planes to Brussels
And I'm with him in Parliament,
When he gets shouted at by Corbyn.
Now you may be asking me,
"What goes on inside his head?"
Okay. I'll tell you,
One time, I got curious,
So I went to have a look,
I waited until he was fast asleep,
Then I went inside his brain
And it was horrifying.

I saw creatures crawling all over the place,
350,000,000 a week, scribbled everywhere,
It shocked me,
But, the worst part was in Brain HQ.
Oh my.
I saw a parasite at the control panel,
Strapped down by iron chains,
I ran like the wind, back to Boris' head.

So yes, Boris is a little mad
And make fun of him all you want,
I don't care,
But don't make fun of me, please,
Because I'm not stupid
And if you make fun of me,
It will make Boris angry,
Really, really angry.

Jonathan Dunn
Wellington School, Ayr

Honey

I was frolicking throughout the meadows,
I noticed a golden hive on the beautiful blossom tree,
Sparkling in the sun were the bees who guarded the
precious treasure,
I walked close up to the tree and sat under the hive,
I noticed a small a hole right underneath, perfect for my
claw to pry it open.
I decided to go for it.
Boom!
The beautiful honey oozed out of the hive but so too did the
angry residents,
I tried to run but I couldn't,
One angry bee accidentally stung me,
She fell down crying and weeping,
"Help, help, help, help, help!"
In her last breath, she said, "So...rr...y..."
I felt so helpless and sorry.
Her family, devastated, cried and wept, over and over again,
I ran away into a cave, pitch-black and dark,
I sat in a corner, wasting away realising I could've been
more sensible but I was hungry and hibernation was near,
I wondered if life would always be like this; horrible winters
and cold-hearted hunters ready to shoot at any moment,
Winter came and I wondered if I could ever warm up but I
was wrong,
I went to sleep and I'm not so sure if I woke up.

Erin Ward
Wellington School, Ayr

Through Their Eyes

Hello,
I'm a Brussel sprout!
I'm most likely to be found in the back of your fridge, old and mouldy,
I've discovered the truth,
It's completely shocking
And I think it'll leave you in a state of shock when I tell you...
Not many people like Brussel sprouts!

Anyways, the fridge I live in is white
And has barely any fruit and veg in it.
Today, the strawberry family had an argument
About whose stalk was the longest...
But, then, the fridge door opened!
"Everybody back into positions!" I heard the milk shout and all went quiet.,
With the blink of an eye, the strawberry family was gone,
Everyone is devastated
And wondering who is going to be next
But I guess I'm used to it.
After all, I've been here for the last three years,
So I know how it goes.

Zoë Rosalyn Glen (11)
Wellington School, Ayr

Tick-Tock

Tick-tock...

Hello? I am here you know,
Sitting here on the wall,
Oh, a quick glance! And away again...
Tick-tock, tick-tock.

I am a clock, as I may have mentioned,
Clocks are here for telling time,
Knowing when to go to work,
Or when you have an important meeting.
Tick-tock, tick-tock.

You see, most people don't really use me anymore,
They have these things called 'mobile phones' which are
obviously more important than me,
Mobile phones tend to do our job, setting alarms and telling
time, no one needs me anymore,
Tick-tock, tick-tock.

Soon enough, I will be gone,
Out of the corner of this house,
The family won't need me, all of them have phones from
what I see,
Tick-tock, tick-tock.

Let's go forward one-hundred years,
Here I am, rotting here,
In the dump with lots of clocks,

No more clocks.
Tick-tock.

Megan Seales (11)
Wellington School, Ayr

I Am A Diary

I am a diary,
My owner writes in me every day,
Her favourite time to write in me is just after she has her
dinner,
Ah! I love dinner- all those words and to top it all off a smile,
She shares everything with me
And I share everything with her.
She takes me everywhere,
In fact, I have been to more than twenty different countries!

I am an old, brown, magical book,
With some of my pages ripped out
And my spine all folded and bent.
I am a little Scottish book,
With little stickers from all over the world on my front page.
They sometimes get a bit annoying when I try to relax.

But, who owns me?
Well, she is a very famous, magical writer,
Have you guessed who it is?
Well, my owner is J.K. Rowling!

Emma Henderson (11)
Wellington School, Ayr

Through Their Eyes

I see the hot bright vibrant red flames,
I see the wounded people walking around like zombies,
I see the planes in the sky as if it was a show.

I feel the sadness,
I feel the fear,
I feel the exhaustion.

I smell the smoke as if the toaster was burning,
I smell the damp air circling around us like a huge, colossal bubble,
I don't smell the fresh, green spring grass anymore.

I feel the sadness,
I feel the fear,
I feel the exhaustion.

I then hear the sirens (as if I wouldn't),
I then hear the explosions that look like fireworks,
I then hear the crying and screaming people that are terrified
And then I hear the footsteps that are coming for us.

I am Anne Frank.

Annabel Elizabeth Barrett (12)
Wellington School, Ayr

The Match

He cleaned the golden Liverpool badge on me,
He put me on his head,
He seemed excited with me.
As his players entered the pitch,
I could tell he was nervous.
As Mané chipped the ball
And the whistle went straight away,
The ref pointed straight to the spot,
The crowd cheered,
As Salah stepped up, he started praying,
That's me on his head,
Salah struck the ball and it flew above the keeper,
It went in and Klopp said, "He's a keeper!"
In a Champions League Final, the Scousers were winning,
He was shaking
And shivering,
Divock finished the game,
The final whistle went,
Klopp went mental
And flew me off his head.

Khalan Thomas Lendrum (12)
Wellington School, Ayr

Through Their Eyes

It's feeling a bit warm today,
Oh, I know what it is,
The stupid girl left my door open again.

What a surprise!
She's back again,
Surely it matters that she was here at,
Ten, fifteen, twenty and now twenty-five minutes past ten.

I would do it myself if I could,
But I can't, so if only someone would,
It's not very nice to have not been cleaned for a year.

You should see the madness,
I don't think anyone could believe it,
But they keep their chocolate in me,
Among other things...
Oh, by the way, I'm a fridge.

Sophia Girgis
Wellington School, Ayr

Winston Churchill's Bowler Hat

I am an important hat,
I sit on top of Churchill's head,
I am not a happy hat,
Being on a head all day.

Churchill's cigar is so rude,
He billows smoke in my face all day,
The dust from bombs always lands on me,
I get achy from sitting still and stiff,
I never get noticed,
I am very stubborn,
I will never listen to anybody.

I am a lonely hat,
I want another hat for company,
I want to be a simple hat to sit on the head of a kind and
caring farmer,
But, instead, I am Winston Churchill's bowler hat
And I need a friend.

Tansy Allan (12)
Wellington School, Ayr

I Must Do My Best

'I must do my best!'

Don't worry about anyone else,
I must do my best.
Focus on my race,
I must do my best.
Just try and get a PB,
I must do my best.

Get in the pool and swim my hardest,
I must do my best.
Don't think about the crowd,
I must do my best.
Give an exciting race,
I must do my best.

Do it for GB,
I must do my best.
Win an Olympic gold,
I must do my best.
I'm the fastest seed,
I must do my best,
No matter what, I must do my best.

Charlotte Hardy (12)
Wellington School, Ayr

Life As My Skates

In the morning,
In the night,
I always see
A wonderful sight,
My sharp blade slicing through
What might just be a block of ice to you,
But in my brain and in my mind
It's something I see, most days you'll find
The glistening ice has just been cleaned,
Or after a day of hard work,
Although, in the corner, Anna likes to lurk,
Every day I see the same feet,
Sliding in and tightening the laces.

Anna Hunter (12)
Wellington School, Ayr

The Door

Rush, rush, rush.
Open. Shut. Open.
It's all the same for me.
Leading to where?
I don't know,
I can't see that way,
I can only see forward.
However, I am old,
I hope I get recycled,
Hope is the only thing I can do.
I hope I am not put in a dump,
I hope not to be leading to a bad place,
I hope not to get knocked down,
I am a door,
I hope you understand me.

Benjamin Richmond
Wellington School, Ayr

Rugby Ball Poem

Hello,
I am going to tell you about my life,
I get kicked,
I get nicked,
I get passed,
I lay on the grass,
I give people points
And watch them break their joints,
I get muck
And I get chucked,
I win matches
And I get scratches,
I roll
And fly between two polls,
I win World Cups
And hear the crowd erupt,
But, what am I?
Can you guess?
I am a rugby ball!

Fraser Steward
Wellington School, Ayr

YOUNG WRITERS INFORMATION

We hope you have enjoyed reading this book – and that you will continue to in the coming years.

If you're a young writer who enjoys reading and creative writing, or the parent of an enthusiastic poet or story writer, do visit our website **www.youngwriters.co.uk**. Here you will find free competitions, workshops and games, as well as recommended reads, a poetry glossary and our blog. There's lots to keep budding writers motivated to write!

If you would like to order further copies of this book, or any of our other titles, then please give us a call or order via your online account.

Young Writers
Remus House
Coltsfoot Drive
Peterborough
PE2 9BF
(01733) 890066
info@youngwriters.co.uk

Join in the conversation!
Tips, news, giveaways and much more!

 YoungWritersUK    @YoungWritersCW